William H. G. Kingston

Janet M'Laren

Or, The Faithful Nurse

William H. G. Kingston

Janet M'Laren
Or, The Faithful Nurse

ISBN/EAN: 9783337059484

Printed in Europe, USA, Canada, Australia, Japan

Cover: Foto ©ninafisch / pixelio.de

More available books at **www.hansebooks.com**

JANET M'LAREN;

OR,

The Faithful Nurse.

BY

WILLIAM H. G. KINGSTON.

———◇———

GALL & INGLIS.

Edinburgh: | London:
BERNARD TERRACE. | 25 PATERNOSTER SQ^R.

CONTENTS.

CHAPTER I.

PAGE

Donald Morrison, whose wife has lately been called away, dying in his Highland Manse, his Children left destitute, are taken care of by their old nurse.—She conveys them to a sea-side town, where she takes up her abode with them in a small attic, and labours for their maintenance, while she places the two boys, Donald and David, at school.—Her anxiety about the education of Margaret, . 11

CHAPTER II.

The boys obtain prizes.—Janet declines receiving visits from Alec Galbraith or any of their school mates.—Margaret's illness.—Is ordered fresh air and sea bathing.—Carried off by a wave, and saved by Alec Galbraith.—Margaret and her brothers are introduced to his mother, 25

CHAPTER III.

PAGE

Mrs Galbraith promises to befriend Margaret.—
Alec's first visit to Janet's attic.—Her schemes
for clothing and supporting the boys.—
Assisted by a kind banker and others.—The
boys make good progress at school.—Janet's
humble faith rewarded, ... 38

CHAPTER IV.

Donald having received an offer from Mr Todd of
an appointment in Canada, accepts it, and
prepares for his departure.—Mrs Galbraith's
unhappiness about her son's religious principles.—Alec, receiving an appointment in
Canada, sails without returning home, to his
mother's and Margaret's grief.—Donald also
leaves home for his destination. . . . 74

CHAPTER V.

PAGE

Donald's voyage to Canada.—He gains the friendship of Mr Skinner.—Reaches Quebec.—
Voyage up the St Lawrence.—Arrival at the
new township.—Description of the settlement.
—Mr Skinner preaches the gospel, and takes
up his residence in the place, ... 60

CHAPTER VI.

Letters from home.—Margaret loses her friend.—
Unsatisfactory report of Alec.—David resolves
to go out.—Donald urges his Sister and Janet
to come also, and prepares for their reception.
No tidings can be obtained of Alec.—David's
arrival.—Mr Skinner explains to him important Gospel truths, ... 74

CHAPTER VII.

Donald's expedition through the forest.—Attacked
by wolves.—Relieved from them by a hurricane, and narrowly escapes being crushed by
falling trees, ... 89

CHAPTER VIII.

PAGE

Donald, resuming his journey, hears a cry of distress.—Finds a man under a fallen tree, who, after carrying him some distance, he discovers to be Alec Galbraith.—Encamp for the night, 98

CHAPTER IX.

When encamped, Donald is visited by an Indian, who assists in carrying Alec to the township. —Influenced by the conduct of the Christian Indians, and the exhortations of his friends, Alec is brought to acknowledge the truth.— His brothers require his presence in England to recover his father's property, and he sets off, ... 106

CHAPTER X.

A letter from Margaret.—Janet's illness.—Anxiety about Alec's return. A delightful surprise. —Arrival of Alec and Margaret, with Janet.

PAGE

Margaret has become Alec's wife.—Conducted
by the brothers to their new house.—Arrival
of Mr Skinner's sister, Mrs Ramsden and her
daughters, who, as might possibly be expected, become the wifes of Donald and
David.—Janet, continuing to live with Margaret, pays frequent visits to her other bairns,
and is ever welcomed by them and the numerous wee bairns who spring up in their midst.
—Conclusion, ...   116

.

JANET M'LAREN;

OR,

The Faithful Nurse.

There stood Margaret and Alexander Galbraith, while dear old
Janet followed close behind.

JANET M'LAREN.

CHAPTER I.

Donald Morrison, whose wife has lately been called away,
    dying in his Highland Manse, his Children left destitute,
    are taken care of by their old nurse.—She conveys them to
    a sea-side town, where she takes up her abode with them
    in a small attic, and labours for their maintenance, while
    she places the two boys, Donald and David, at school.—
    Her anxiety about the education of Margaret.

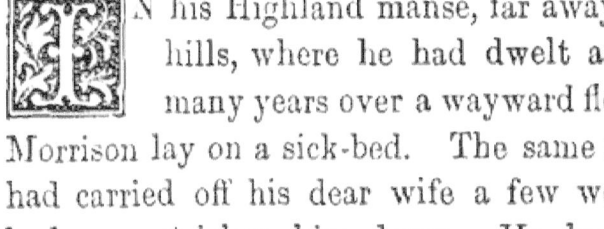N his Highland manse, far away among the
hills, where he had dwelt as pastor for
many years over a wayward flock, Donald
Morrison lay on a sick-bed. The same fever which
had carried off his dear wife a few weeks before,
had now stricken him down. He knew that he
was dying. As far as he himself was concerned he
was willing to yield up his spirit to his Maker; but
what would become of his motherless children, his
sweet young Margaret, and his two boys, Donald
and David, their principles unformed, and ignorant
of the evils of the world?

'Father in heaven protect them,' he ejaculated. 'Give me faith to know that Thou wilt take care of them, teach them and guide them in their course through life.' But he felt that his mind was clouded, his spirit was cast down, the disease was making rapid progress. It was hard to think, hard even to pray, gloomy ideas, and doubts, and fears, such as assail even true Christians, crowded on his mind. He forgot—it was but for a time—the sincere faith which had animated him through life. The victory was not to be with the Evil One.

Soon there came hope, and joy, and confidence. 'All will be well with the righteous, those who put on Christ's righteousness,' he mentally exclaimed, and peace came back to his soul.

As he gazed out through the window he could see, down away on the wild hill side, his children at play, their young spirits too buoyant to be long suppressed by the recollection of their late bereavement, and unconscious that they were soon to be deprived of their remaining parent. His eye for a moment rested on the familiar landscape, the blue waters of the loch glittering in the sunshine, a bleak moorland sprinkled here and there with white-fleeced sheep stretching away on one side, and on the other a valley, down which flowed, with ceaseless murmurings, a rapid stream, a steep hill covered with gorse and heather, the summit crowned with a wood of dark pines rising beyond it. Just above the manse could be seen the kirk, which, with a few cottages, composed the village ; while scattered far around were the huts in which the larger part of the pastor's flock abode. As he gazed forth on the scene he prayed—he knew it might be for the last time—that his successor might be more honoured than he feared he had been in bringing home those wandering sheep to the true fold.

Once more his thoughts turned to his little ones. ' Janet,' he whispered, as a woman of middle age, of spare form, with strongly marked features, be-tokening firmness and good sense, and clothed in the humblest style of attire, glided noiselessly into the room. ' I feel that I am going.' He lifted up his pale and shrivelled hand, and pointed to his children, ' What is to become of them, it is hard to leave them destitute, utterly destitute, not a friend in the world from whom they may claim assistance.'

' Dinna talk so, minister,' said the woman, approaching him, and placing his arm beneath the bed-clothes. ' Ye yoursel have often told us to put faith in God, that He is the Father of the father-less, and the husband of the widow. The dear bairns will nay want while He looks after them. I hanna dwelt forty years or more with the mistress that's gone, and her sainted mother before her, to desert those she has left behind, while I ha' finger to work with, and eyes to see. I'll never forget either to impress on their minds all the lessons you have taught me. It would have been little worth ganging to kirk if I had not remembered them too. I am a poor weak body mysel, it will not be me but He who watches over us will do it, let that comfort you, minister. The bairns will never be so badly off as ye are thinking, now that fever has made body and soul weak, but the soul will soon recover, and ye will rejoice with joy unspeakable. I repeat but your ain words, minister, and I ken they are true.'

'Ye are right, Janet. My soul is reviving,' whispered the dying man. 'Call in the bairns. I would have them round me once more. The end is near.'

Janet knew that her master spoke too truly; though it grieved her loving heart to put a stop to the play of the happy young creatures, and to bring them to a scene of sorrow and death. 'But it maun be,' she said to herself, as she went to the door of the manse. 'He who kens all things kens what is best, and the minister is ganging away from his toils and troubles here to that happy home up there, where he will meet the dear mistress, and, better still, be with Him who loved him, and shed His blood to redeem him, as he himsel has often and often told us from the pulpit.'

She went some way down the hill, unwilling to utter her usual shrill call to the young ones. 'Ye maun come in now, bairns,' she said, in a gentle

tone ; when the children came running up on seeing
her beckoning. 'The minister is sair ill, and ye'll
be good and quiet, and listen to what he says to
you, he is ganging awa on a long long journey, and
ye'll promise to do what he'll tell you till ye are
called to the same place he'll reach ere lang.'

Something in her tone struck Margaret, who
took her hand, and looking up into her face burst
into tears. She already knew what death was.
Donald, the eldest boy, had lingered a short distance behind.

David, seeing Margaret's tears, with a startled,
anxious look, took Janet's other hand. 'Is father
ganging to heaven?' he asked, as they got close to
the house, showing how his mind had been occupied as they came along.

'I am sure of it, and it is a happy, happy place,'
was the answer. 'Ye'll speak gently, Donald,' she
said, turning round to the eldest boy, who, ignorant
of his father's state, might not, she feared, restrain
his exuberant spirits.

There was no need of the caution, for the minister's altered look struck even Donald with awe.
Janet led the children up to the bedside. The
dying father stretched out his hands, and placed
them on their heads, as they clustered up to him,
while his already dim eyes turned a fond glance at
their young fresh faces. 'You will listen to Janet
when I am away, and pray God to help you to meet

me in heaven. Make His word your guide, and you cannot mistake the road.' ' I will try to mind that, and tell Donald and David, too,' was all that Margaret could answer.

' Canna ye stay longer with us, father?' asked Donald, touching the minister's hand, as he was wont to do when speaking to him.

' He we should all obey has called me,' said Mr Morrison. ' May He bless you, and guard and keep you. Bless you! bless you!' His voice was becoming fainter and fainter, and so he died, with his hands on his children's heads, his loving eyes on their cherub faces.

' Blessed are they who die in the Lord,' said Janet, as she observed the smile which seemed to rest on the minister's features. Taking the children, scarcely yet conscious of what had occurred, she led them from the room, and then stepped back to close the eyes of the dead.

Having put the sobbing orphans to bed, she hastened out to obtain the assistance of a neighbour in preparing the body for burial. She insisted on paying the woman for the office she had performed, remarking, as she did so, ' I have the charge of the manse and the bairns till the minister's friends come to take them awa', and they would na' wish to be beholden to any one, or to leave any of his lawful debts unpaid.' In the same way she took upon herself the arrangement and expense of the funeral. She sold the goods and chattels, as her master had directed her to do, for the benefit of his children ; but they were old and worn, and the purchasers were few and poor, so that the proceeds placed but a very limited sum in Janet's hands for the maintenance of the little ones. As she received them she observed, ' It's as muckle as I could ha' hoped for ; but yet those who had benefited by his ministrations might have shown their gratitude by geeing a trifle above the value for the chattels.' Human nature is much the same in an Highland glen as it is in other parts of the world.

The day arrived when Janet and her charges must quit the manse. She had sent up to Jock M'Intyre, the carrier, to call for the kist which contained her's and the children's clothing, as he passed down the glen. The most weighty article was the minister's Bible, with which, although it might have brought more than anything else, she would not part. She had reserved also a few other books for the children's instruction.

Taking Margaret and David by the hand, Donald leading the way with a bundle of small valuables over his shoulder, she set forth from the house which had sheltered her for many long years, into the cold world. Margaret's eyes were filled with tears, and David cast many a longing glance behind him, while Donald, with his bundle, trudged steadily on with his gaze ahead, as if he was eager to overtake something in the distance. Whatever thoughts were passing in his mind he did not make them known.

Janet's head was bent slightly forward, her countenance calm, almost stern. A difficult task was before her, and she meant, with God's grace, to perform it. She had not told the children where she was going, though she had made up her own mind on the subject. Several of the cottagers came out to bid them farewell; but as she had made cronies of none of them, there was little exhibition of feeling, and she had taken good care that no one should be aware of the destitute condition in which the orphans were left. Humble presents and offers of assistance would undoubtedly have been made, but Janet shrunk from the feeling that her charges should be commiserated by those among whom their parents had lived, and she returned but brief thanks to the farewells offered her. She would far rather have been left to pursue her way without interruption. 'Fare-ye-weel, neighbours, just tack Miss Margaret's, and the laddies, and my ain thanks, but we canna delay, for Jock will be spearing for us, and we ha' a lang journey to make before nightfall,' she said, bending her head towards one and the other as she wended her way among them down the hill side.

Janet had a horror of cities and towns, having been bred and lived all her life in the Highlands, with the exception of a brief visit she once paid, with Mrs Morrison's mother, to beautiful ———, on the east coast. It being the only town with which she was acquainted, she had made up her mind to go there.

She had heard also that there was a school in the place, and to that school Donald and David must forthwith be sent. Without learning, she was well aware, she could not expect them to get on in the world as she wished. With regard to Margaret, the consideration of how she was to be brought up in a way befitting a young lady, caused her more anxiety than anything else. She might, indeed, teach her many useful things, but she was herself incompetent, she felt, to train the little damsel's manners, or to give her instruction from books. Still, ' where there's a will there's a way,' she said to herself, ' and I ha' a tongue in my head, and that tongue I can wag whenc'er it can do the bairns good.'

The journey was a long one, and though honest Jock charged but little for their conveyance, a large hole was made in Janet's means before they arrived at the end of it.

The gaunt grave woman, with her three fresh blooming children, caused some curiosity, as she went about looking for lodgings. A single upper room was all she could venture to engage. Here she took up her quarters with her young charges, and thanking her merciful Father who had brought her thus far in safety, she felt like a hen which had safely gathered her brood under her wings. She furnished her abode with two truckle-beds, one for the boys, the other for Margaret and herself. She procured also a small table and four three-legged stools, a similar number of mugs and plates, and a few other inexpensive articles.

That same evening, determined not to lose a moment of time, with well used spinning-wheel set up, she began to spin away as if she had been long settled, while the children played around her, glad once more to find themselves alone, and free from the gaze of strangers. She waited till they were asleep, and then set to work, to manufacture out of the minister's best suit some fresh garments for the boys, such as she considered befitting their condition. Her busy needle was going the greater part of the night, still she was up betimes, and again at work. She, however, allowed the children to sleep on as long as they would. 'They will weary up here in this sma' room, the poor bairns, instead of running about on their aine free heathery hills, and I must na' spare the time to take them out on the links just now till their clays are ready, and I can send them to school.'

One of those admirable institutions in Scotland for the education of all classes enabled Janet to carry out her project without difficulty. Mr and Mrs Morrison had carefully taught their children, and the two boys were well advanced for their age. The master of the school, on hearing who they were, at once received the orphans, and promised, as far as he could, to befriend them. 'If you will be obedient boys, and try and say your lessons well, you will get on,' he observed.

Donald looked him full in the face, and at once said he would try, and he always meant what he said. David made no answer, but clung to Janet's gown, as if unwilling to be left behind among so many strange people.

'Ye will be back in the afternoon, and we will be spearing for you, bairns,' she said. 'They are precious, sir, very precious,' she added, turning to the master. 'If they are shown the right way, as their father showed it them, they will walk in it; but the deil's a cunning deceiver, and ever ganging about to get hold of young souls as weel as old ones. Ye'll doubtless warn them, and keep them out of bad company.'

'I'll do my best, my good woman,' answered the master, struck at Janet's earnestness for the interests of her charges; and having bid her farewell, he led off Donald and David, while Janet, taking Margaret by the hand, returned to her lodging to resume her daily labour, well satisfied with the arrangements she had made for the education of the two boys.

Donald and David returned safe home in the evening from their first day at school. Donald was full of all he had seen and done, and was especially delighted at finding that he was superior to many boys of his own age. Having made several friends, he said he thought school a very fine place. He might have gone out to play a game of golf on the links, and he would have done so had he not promised Janet to return at once, but he hoped that she would let him go another day. David had not been behind hand with his brother in his class, but he had not been so happy, and the boys had asked him questions to which he had been unable to frame replies, without betraying the truth, which Janet had especially charged them not to do.

'They wanted to ken all about us,' exclaimed Donald, and I told them that they must just mind their ain business; my home might be a castle in the Highlands some day, and whatever it might now be, I was contented with it.'

'A very proper answer,' exclaimed Janet, smiling for the first time for many a long day. 'Ye maunna be ashamed of your home, or those in it, laddie; just gang on doing your duty, but dinna mind what young or old, or rich or poor, think of ye.'

'But I said nothing, I would na answer them,' said David, sobbing.

'Ye did weel, too, laddie,' observed Janet. 'The

wise man knows where his strength lies, the weakest may thus come off the conqueror.'

She had now to make arrangements for Margaret's education. This was more difficult than for that of the boys. She could not trust her sweet, gentle, blue-eyed maid among girls who might be rough or unmannerly, and yet she could not possibly afford to send her to one of the upper class of schools. Margaret already read much better than she did, for her own attainments extended no further than a limited amount of reading and writing. The few books, besides the Bible, she had brought away from the minister's library, were mostly on theological subjects, somewhat, she felt sure, beyond Margaret's comprehension. She lived on dry crusts for many a day to sanction her extravagance in purchasing several books, one after the other, suited to the little maiden's taste. Margaret was delighted to receive them, and while Janet sat and span she read them aloud to her, and amply rewarded was the kind nurse for her self-denial. Not dreaming that Margaret could possibly educate herself, she still continued turning in her mind how that desirable object should be accomplished.

'Dinna ye think that if we ask God He will show us the way,' said Margaret, one day, looking up into the face of her nurse, who had made some remark on the subject.

'We will do as ye propose, my sweet bairn.

answered Janet. ' He is sure to hear us,' and, accordingly, when the chapter from the Bible had been read, which Janet never omitted doing, she, with her young flock around her, knelt in prayer, as had been the custom at the manse, and she did not fail to ask for guidance and direction in the matter which had so sorely perplexed her mind.

CHAPTER II.

The boys obtain prizes.—Janet declines receiving visits from Alec Galbraith, or any of their school mates.—Margaret's illness.—Is ordered fresh air and sea bathing.—Carried off by a wave, and saved by Alec Galbraith.—Margaret and her brothers are introduced to his mother.

IT gave joy to the loving heart of Janet, when one day her two bairns came home, each with a prize under his arm.

'But mine is only the second in my form; David got the first prize in his,' said Donald, as they exhibited their books to the eager eyes of their nurse and sister.

'Weel, they are bonny—they are bonny,' exclaimed Janet, as still mechanically spinning away, she bent over the books which Margaret, with sisterly eagerness, was examining.

'I thought I should have had the first, but another fellow ran me hard and gained it,' said Donald.

'Who was he?' asked Margaret, looking up, inclined to quarrel with the boy who had deprived
her brother of the honour which she thought ought
to have been his.

'A very fine fellow—one Alec Galbraith—he
beat me fairly ; and there's as much in him as any
boy at school.' Margaret felt that she had been too
hasty in her conclusions. 'I intended to bring him
here for you to see, Margaret,' continued Donald.
'Though he lives in a fine house, and has a father
and mother, and several big brothers away in foreign
parts, I am not going to let him suppose that I am
ashamed of my home. He has often asked me, and
I am determined to be able to say, "That's where I
live, and now what do you think of me ?"'

'Nay, nay, my bairn, dinna ye bring him here,'
exclaimed Janet. She thought she knew more of
the world than her young charge, and scarcely comprehended his independent spirit, though her own
in reality was very similar. 'He will just be laughing at you afterwards, and tell others that ye live
in an attic with a poor old woman.'

'He had better not,' exclaimed Donald, in an
angry tone. 'But I ken he will na do ony sic
thing—he is an honest fellow, and if he likes me it
is for what I am, and not for where I live.'

'Dinna ask Galbraith to come here,' put in
David. 'Though he may be the same to you, he
may be letting out to others, and maybe they will

ne'er be so kind in their remarks, and will be asking to come here themselves.'

This last observation of David's decided Janet. ' We will ne'er have Alec Galbraith, nor any other of your school-mates, coming here, Donald, so just tell them that Janet M'Laren does not wish to receive visitors,' she exclaimed, in a more authoritative tone than she usually employed. Donald promised to act as she desired, and Alec Galbraith continued to be known only by name to her and Margaret.

Although the two boys, in consequence of the active life they led going to and from school, and playing on the open links, retained their health, Margaret, unaccustomed to the confinement to which she was subjected, began to grow thin and pale. Her cheeks lost their bloom, her spirit, and the joyous elasticity of her step, were gone. Janet at length perceived the change in the sweet child, and saw that something must be done for her. She took her to a doctor, who advised fresh air, with a romp every day on the links, and sea-bathing. The remedies were cheap ; but Janet could not think of allowing Margaret to go out without her, and she could not afford the time unless she took out her knitting-needles, which usually employed her fingers when her spinning-wheel was laid aside.

The next morning the old Highland woman was

to be seen pacing the links, knitting as she walked, while Margaret, delighted with her newly gained freedom, went bounding away before her, only wishing that she had her brothers to share her happiness. When they came home in the evening she easily persuaded Janet to go out again ; and as the three children set off together, they felt as they had not since they left their Highland home. Still, as the doctor had prescribed bathing, Janet, who had paid for the advice, considered that it would be throwing away the siller if it was not carried out.

The maidens, of high and low degree, in that unpretending little town, both then and long after, were accustomed to enjoy the salt water in a primitive fashion. Neither tents nor bathing machines were thought of. Each matron stood ready with a large sheet, under which her charge put on her bathing-dress, and then ran off to frolic amid the waves, resuming her wonted garments in the same way, after her bath. Margaret, till now, had never seen the ocean. It inspired no fear—only delight and pleasure—and she hurried into the water like a sea nymph, enjoying its bracing freshness. For many successive mornings she went down, in company with several other girls of various ages, to bathe and sport with glee in the bright waters of a little bay, sheltered on either side by high rocks from the gaze of passers by.

One morning the sea, though still bright, came rolling in with greater force than usual, dashing the sparkling spray high up against the dark rocks. Several of the other girls exclaimed that they should enjoy a delightful bath, and Janet, unaware of the treacherous character of the ocean, did not hesitate to allow Margaret to join them. Now a wave came rolling in, sweeping in a snowy sheet of foam high up the beach, now it receded with a murmuring sound over the rounded pebbles. The girls, taking each other's hands, ventured in as far as they were accustomed to go, waiting till they saw a wave approaching, when they hurried back again up the beach, where they could escape its force. Margaret, as the last comer, was the outer one of the line. Not comprehending the necessity of caution, she let go her companion's hand at the moment the rest of the party were making their escape from the coming sea. In an instant she felt herself lifted off her feet; she endeavoured to spring forward, but the wave had her in its grasp, and, as with a loud roar it receded, she was carried away towards the entrance of the bay.

For the first moment Janet did not perceive the danger of her darling. ' Oh my bairn ! my bairn !' she shrieked out, when she discovered what had occurred, and throwing down the sheet she rushed into the water vainly attempting to reach her. Several of the elder girls, horror-stricken, held her back, scarcely conscious of what they were doing. Louder and louder she raised her imploring cries for help, as she endeavoured to break loose from the agitated group surrounding her.

Margaret continued floating on the surface ; but was every instant being borne further away towards the white-topped waves which rose outside the bay. At that instant a lad was seen to run along the top of the rocks till he neared the end, when, without a moment's hesitation, he sprung off into the water, and swam boldly towards the little girl. She had not from the first struggled, and she lay perfectly quiet, while he grasped her dress with one hand and struck out with the other towards the beach. The danger of both was great. Now they appeared to have made good progress, and now the sea carried them out again towards the mouth of the bay ; but the lad still swam on with undaunted courage towards the eager arms which were stretched out to assist him in landing. At length he succeeded in getting near enough to allow Janet to grasp her charge, and once having her in her arms, she bore her away up the beach to a warm nook under the rocks, while the lad, his task accomplished, made good his footing, and then, without waiting to receive the congratulations of the girls, and the thanks which Janet would have poured out, hurried off towards his home to change his wet clothing.

Margaret, who had fainted, quickly returned to consciousness; and from the remarks she made while Janet was putting on her dry clothing, she seemed scarcely aware of what had occurred, nor till the other girls, who had speedily dressed, gathered round her, did she understand the danger in which she had been placed.

'Who is he? Can ony o' ye tell me the brave laddie's name? that I may thank him and love him for saving my bairn,' asked Janet. Some of the girls gave one name, some another.

'Na, na, he is neither o' them,' exclaimed one of the elder girls. 'He is young Alec Galbraith, whose father and mother live in the big house over the links there. He gangs to the school, and my brothers ken him weel.'

Taking her bairn in her arms, Janet hastened homewards. The boys had already started for school, ignorant of the danger to which their sister had been exposed. Janet placed her on the bed, and now, for the first time, giving way to her feelings, burst into tears. 'I'll ne'er again trust you to that treacherous sea, my own sweet bairn,' she exclaimed, bending over her. 'If it had taken you away, I could na have lived to come home and see the poor boys breaking their hearts, and they would have had no one left to care for them. But our God is kind and merciful, and we maun lift up our hearts to Him in praise and thanksgiving.'

' I will try to do so, dear Janet, though I feel that I cannot be grateful enough to Him,' said Margaret, in a faint voice, and comprehending perhaps now far more than before, from the unusual agitation of her nurse, the fearful peril through which she had been preserved. ' And, Janet,' she added, in a whisper, ' I should like to thank, with my whole heart, the brave boy who swam out to me and brought me safely on shore. I remember seeing him running along the rocks and coming towards me, and then I felt sure I was safe.'

' Yes, we will thank him. If I had to live a hundred years, I would thank him to the end of my days,' exclaimed Janet. But his parents are rich people, and a poor body like me can give him ne'er more than empty thanks.'

' But if they come from the bottom of our hearts he'll prize them,' observed Margaret. ' And do ye ken who he is?'

' Aye, that I do—he is Donald's class-mate, no other than Alec Galbraith, your brother is always talking about.'

' Oh, I am so glad,' exclaimed Margaret. ' I can believe all Donald says of him. I must go with you and thank him too, and I will never more be jealous though he keeps at the head of the class, and Donald is only second. He must be as brave as he is clever, or he would not have risked his life to save that of a poor little stranger girl like me, and then to have gone away without even stopping to be thanked.'

Janet guessed that young Galbraith was not likely at that time to be found at his house, and indeed Margaret was not fit to go out again at present. She therefore waited till the boys came home in the evening from school. They had heard nothing of what had occurred. All they knew was, that Alec Galbraith had come later than usual to school, that the master had received his excuses, and that he had performed his tasks with even more than his ordinary ability. They listened with panting breath to the account Janet gave of the occurrence.

'Bless him,' cried Donald, 'I will never again try to take him down. I would rather he had done it than any other fellow in the school.'

'I will give him all my prizes, and pray for him as long as I live,' exclaimed David.

Janet thought Margaret sufficiently recovered in the evening to venture out. 'We must go with you,' exclaimed Donald. 'I want to take Galbraith by the hand, and tell him all I feel.'

The party set off—Janet, as usual, taking her knitting as she quitted her wheel, from which her active fingers had been spinning yarn even while the conversation above described had been going on. Margaret was rather pale, and somewhat weak, but her sturdy brothers supported her on either side.

C

Though she was eager to thank Alec Galbraith, she felt somewhat timid at the thoughts of encountering him and his parents.

'I know Alec well enough to be sure that he will make light of the matter,' observed Donald. 'He will tell you that he ran no danger, and enjoyed the swim. But that must not make us less grateful to him. I do not know what sort of people his parents are—perhaps high and mighty, and may be angry with you for placing their son in danger. However, I don't care what they say; nothing shall make any difference in my feelings towards Alec.'

'Nor in mine either,' whispered Margaret.

'Nor in mine,' said David. 'I only wish that I had more to offer him, not that I can ever pay him, but just to show my love and gratitude.

Would that people were as grateful to God for the benefits daily received, and above all, to Jesus, for the great salvation He has wrought for us, as these young people were to the brave boy who had risked his life to save that of little Margaret.

The above conversation took place as they approached the handsome residence of Mr Galbraith. Alec had seen them. He ran out to meet his friends. 'I am so glad you have come, Donald. My mother wants to know you—for I have often told her about you, and how hard you pressed me in the class. And is this little girl your sister? Why!' and he looked up from Margaret to Janet, and blushed, as if he had done something to be ashamed of. 'I do believe that I had the pleasure of towing you on shore this morning; but don't talk about it—it was no trouble at all, and I have often wetted these old clothes through and through before.'

'Oh, but I maun talk about it,' exclaimed Janet, grasping his hands, and pouring out her thanks with all the impetuosity which her grateful feelings prompted.

'I knew that was what you would say, Alec,' exclaimed Donald. 'But we know better about the danger and trouble. You might have been carried away by the sea, for I am very sure you would never have let go of Maggie while you had life.'

Margaret tried to say something, but she could never exactly remember what words she uttered.

'If there was any danger, I am sure I did not think about it,' said Alec. 'And I am very glad, for your sakes that we got safe to shore. But now come in and see my mother, for I have often told her that as you would not let me go to pay you a visit, we must get you to come here.'

Mrs Galbraith, a very amiable and gentle looking woman, received her visitors with the greatest kindness, and tried at once to make Janet at home. The old nurse expressed to her the gratitude

she felt to her young son for the service he had
rendered.

' It is indeed a happiness to me to find that my
boy has behaved rightly and bravely,' answered the
lady. ' It would have been a sad thing if the life
of that sweet little girl had been lost, and I can only
rejoice that my dear boy was the means of preserving it. I should like to become better acquainted with her, and you will, I hope, allow her and
her brothers to remain here. I'll send them home
at night, or perhaps you would like to come for
them.

' I'll come for them, mem, and am grateful to
you for your kindness,' said Janet, who dreaded any
one visiting her humble abode, while, at the same
time her heart beat with satisfaction at the hope
that at length her dear little Margaret might obtain a friend who would give her that assistance
in her education which she herself was unable to
afford.

Leaving the children with their new friends, she
cheerfully went to her solitary home to sit and spin,
and think over what might be their future fate in
life ; and as she span many were the schemes she
drew out in her imagination of their destiny. The
boys would do well she was sure, though they might
have a hard tussel with the world. Donald would
do battle bravely with any foes he might have to
encounter, and David would not be behind hand,

although he might meet them in a more quiet manner. Maybe he will wish to follow in the steps of his father, and become a minister of the gospel, she thought. Weel, weel, its a true saying, that ' Man proposes, and God disposes.' If we trust in Him all will be for the best.

CHAPTER III.

Mrs Galbraith promises to befriend Margaret.—Alec's first visit to Janet's attic.—Her schemes for clothing and supporting the boys.—Assisted by a kind banker and others.—The boys make good progress at school.—Janet's humble faith rewarded.

HE children had a great deal to tell of all they had seen at Mistress Galbraith's when Janet came to take them home.

'She is, indeed, a very kind lady,' said Margaret. 'She told me that once she had a little daughter just like me, but God had taken her to Himself, and asked me if I would like to come and see her very often ; but I said that I couldna leave you, Janet, all alone, when the boys were at school, with no one to talk to you.'

'I can talk to myself, Margaret, ye ken,' answered Janet. 'I would na hae ye say nae to the good lady, for I like her looks and her way of speaking, and she may be a true friend to ye. And

38

if she asks you again ye will just say ye will do what she pleases, and that ye are obliged to her. And what do you think of the big house and the great people?' she asked, turning to Donald.

'It's all very braw and fine; but I would rather hae a house of my ain, and you in it, Janet,' answered Donald.

'May be you will get that, laddie, some day.'

'I hope I may; and then I'll ask Alec to come and stay with me, since you will na let him come here,' said Donald.

'I could na deny him onything—so, if he wishes to come, he must come,' said Janet.

'Then I will tell him,' said Donald, 'and I am sure he will not carry tales to the other boys.

The next morning Alec found out the house on his road to school, and made his way up to Janet's attic. He tapped gently at the door. Donald went out to meet him.

'I told you we did not live in a fine house, and so you see,' he observed, pointing round the room. 'But I am sure you do not think the worse of us, or our good nurse. We should have been starving if it was not for her—that's what I have got to tell you.'

'No, indeed, I do not think the worse of you or her,' answered Alec. 'If I thought it would vex you I would not have come; and I promise you that I will not say a word to others which you would not wish me to say. But my mother desired me to call and invite your sister Margaret to spend the day with her, if Mistress Janet will give her leave.'

'She will go, and gladly, as soon as the boys are off to school,' said Janet, answering at once for Margaret.

'Come along then,' exclaimed Alec to his companions. 'My mother is longing to see Miss Margaret again, and we will not delay her.'

As soon as the boys were away Janet set off with her charge. Mrs Galbraith received her with the greatest kindness, and would have had Janet to stay with her also.

'Thank ye, Mistress Galbraith,' answered Janet. 'But I ha' my household affairs to attend to, and they will na get on very weel unless I am present.'

From that day forward Janet escorted Margaret to the house of her new friend every morning at the same hour.

Janet greatly missed her young companion, but she sat on in her solitude rejoicing in the thought that Margaret was gaining the instruction she so much desired her to obtain. As she span and span she turned in her mind various plans for supporting the children and for ultimately establishing them in life.

Their claithes will soon be worn out. Donald

is already too big for his, and though they may do
for David for a few months longer, with patching
and mending, I would na' like to ha' the poor boys
pointed out by their school mates as young gaber-
lunzies ; and the siller I get for the yarn will only
just pay the rent and find porridge for the bairns,'
she thought to herself. 'The Bible says that it is
the duty of Christians to support the fatherless and
widows. I would na' beg for mysel' while I ha'
got fingers to spin wee, but I maun nay let my
pride stand in the way o' the bairns. They maun
be clothed and fed, so I need find out those who
ha' got the means, and gi'e them the privilege of
helping the young orphans. The good lady, Mistress Galbraith, will look after Margaret, I ha' little
fear o' that, but I canna let her ha' the charge of
the boys.'

Janet having made up her mind to act never
lost time in setting about it. As yet she was unacquainted with the names of any of the people in
the place, with the exception of Margaret's new
friend. This knowledge she had to gain ; but, as
she said to herself, 'wi' a tongue in her mouth,
and lugs to listen wee, that was na' a difficult
matter.'

She first visited the few shops at which she
dealt, and getting into conversation with the masters or mistresses, quickly gleaned from them some
of the desired information. Having, with much

acuteness, made up her mind as to those most likely to respond to her appeal, she went forth the next morning, having deposited Margaret with Mrs Galbraith, to commence the series of visits she proposed making.

The first was to Mr M'Tavish, the banker, an elder in the church, and a man much respected, she heard. He listened to her tale with his keen eyes fixed on her countenance. 'You speak the truth,' he said at length, putting his hand in his pocket and drawing out his purse.

'Na, na, sir, I dinna want the siller,' said Janet. 'If you ha' a mind, sir, to gie a jacket or a pair of breeks to the minister's son, or ony other article of dress ye think fit, I'll be grateful, but I dinna come to beg. It must be a free gift on your part. I dinna want any man's siller.'

The banker, somewhat amused at the good woman's reply, promised to supply Donald with a new suit; and writing an order to his clothier, desired her to present it, and obtain what she wanted. Highly delighted with her success she took Donald in the evening to be measured for a suit, having first begged the master not to allow the boy to know how it was obtained.

'Its not that I would na' wish him to be thankful, but it would be bad for him to feel that he is supported by charity. And I will pray for blessings on the head of the good gentleman, and the day

may come when he is able to show that he is
sensible of his kindness,' she observed.

The worthy clothier appreciated her motives.
'You have another bairn, I understand, to look
after,' he observed. 'When he is in want of a
suit let me know, and I will try what I can do for
him.'

Janet thanked him for his kindness, and promised not to forget his offer.

She was not always so successful as in these
first instances. Some people refused to believe her
story, or declared that they had already more people
looking to them for assistance than they could support; others again gave full credit to her tale, and
admiring her faithfulness and honesty, were glad of
an opportunity of helping the destitute orphans of
whom she had nobly taken charge. Frequently
she brought home a supply of food, but not a
particle of it would she touch herself. 'It was
given for the fatherless bairns, and they alone have
the right to it,' she would say, contenting herself
with a bowl of brose, the usual coarse fare on which
she subsisted.

The sale of her yarn enabled her to pay her
rent, and to find food for herself, and a portion for
the children. Her own rough garments appeared never to wear out, while the roof of a neighbouring house below the window of her attic
afforded her a drying ground on washing days.

Money she would never receive; but as the history of the orphans became known, she was amply supplied with clothing for them of all descriptions.

Donald and David continued to make excellent progress at school, obtaining the approbation of all their masters, and gaining, in addition to Alec Galbraith, several friends among their school mates.

'Your boys, if they continue as they have begun, are sure to do well, Mrs M'Laren,' said the head-master, when she went to pay their school fees.

'Weel, sir, I am sure too o' that, for the prayers of the minister and my dear mistress could na' have been offered in vain, and though I am but an humble woman, it is the chief thing I ask o' God, and I ken He will na' refuse my request.'

Margaret went daily to Mrs Galbraith, but that lady did not offer to take her entirely under her charge. She had her reasons for this; her own health was failing, and she felt that should she be taken away, and the young girl be again thrown back on Janet's hands she would feel the change more than if she continued to reside with her kind nurse. Although she had never visited Janet, she guessed the limited accommodation her attic must afford, and had, therefore, engaged, giving Janet the money to pay the rent, another small chamber on the same floor, which was devoted to the use of the two boys. Janet gladly accepted the offer. She felt that as the children were growing up such an arrangement was absolutely necessary for their comfort, though it might have been beyond her means to supply it.

When the days shortened the two boys might have been seen in their little room, seated on their three-legged stools, with a table, manufactured by themselves, between them, their heads bent down close together over their books, to obtain as much light as the farthing candle, placed in the most advantageous position, could afford. When the cold of winter came on they were compelled to seek Janet's fire-side, where she would sit silent as a mouse, watching them with fond eyes, as they conned their tasks, while Margaret, on the other side, actively plied her needle, either making her own clothes, or performing some work for her kind patroness. Margaret had lost the bloom of childhood, and though her features were not sufficiently regular to allow her to be considered decidedly pretty, she had grown into an interesting girl, with an amiable expression of countenance—a faithful index of her mind. Donald had become a strong active fine looking lad, with features which betokened firmness and decision of character, while David, though not so robust as his brother, was

handsomer, and a stranger, seeing the two together, would at once have pronounced him pos-
sessed of more mildness and gentleness than his
elder brother, and less able to buffet with the
rude world.

CHAPTER IV.

Donald having received an offer from Mr Todd of an appointment in Canada, accepts it, and prepares for his departure.
—Mrs Galbraith's unhappiness about her son's religious
principles.—Alec receiving an appointment in Canada,
sails without returning home, to his mother's and Margaret's
grief.—Donald also leaves home for his destination.

JANET and David were the sole occupants
of the attic. The lad was seated at his
little table with his books and papers
before him, Janet looking on wondering at the
strange figures he rapidly formed as he worked
away at his mathematical studies. The weather
was still cold, and she had pressed him to keep her
company, and enjoy the warmth of her fire, which
the early season rendered necessary. Not a word
had she uttered lest it might interrupt him, when,
as she drew forth the thread from her wheel, which
had been idle but a few hours out of the twenty-
four, Sabbath days excepted, since her arrival at
her present abode, David looked up and inquired
how many yards she could spin in a minute.

'I ne'er thought anent it,' she answered. 'But
why do ye ask, my bairn?'

47

'Because I wish to calculate how many times the yarn you have spun since we came here would encircle the globe,' answered David.

'Oh, but to be sure a puir body like o' me could na' do sic a thing as that,' she exclaimed, rather aghast at the very idea of such a performance. David, however, marking the yarn with his pen, bade her spin away while he counted sixty.

He was engaged in his calculations when a quick eager step was heard on the stair, and Donald, his countenance glowing with health and animation, entered the room.

'Janet, I have had an offer, a magnificent offer,' he exclaimed, breathless from some other cause beyond the mere effort of mounting the stairs. 'I would consult no one, and would tell no one till I had seen you. I was playing at golf on the links, when, rushing along, I ran right against a gentleman who was standing watching the game. I stopped to beg his pardon, when, looking up in his face, I was sure he was Mr Todd, he who was grieve o' the laird of Glenvarlock, and used to come often to the manse and ha' a crack with our father. Many is the time he has carried me in front of him on his horse, and lent me a pony to ride. I asked him— I was right—I told him my name, and that I was at the High School here, and Margaret and David and I were living with you. He shook me warmly by the hand, and said he was very glad to meet with me, inquiring what I thought of doing, and many other questions. He then begged, as soon as the game was over, that I would accompany him to his lodgings. "I have been thinking of something for you, Donald," he said, when I rejoined him. "I am preparing to start, as soon as the spring commences, at the head of a party of emigrants to settle on a large tract of land in Upper Canada, and I want the assistance of one or two active young men, with heads on their shoulders, who have their way to make in the world. I have been out there for two years, and know the wants of the country. Active surveyors are especially required, and I can assure you that you will be able to obtain a sufficient knowledge of surveying, for all practical purposes, before we start. All your expenses will be paid, and you will receive a small salary to commence with. Say that you will accompany me, and I will not look elsewhere for an assistant." I told him I could not say yes till I had asked you, Janet, and talked to Margaret and David. I do not like to leave you all, but you see I may make my fortune, and have a home for you all to come to some day; and if I stay in Scotland it may be long before I can obtain a situation, and longer still before I can have a house of my own.'

Janet remained silent for some minutes, gazing fondly at Donald, revolving the matter in her mind,

D

with her lips apart as if the announcement had taken away her breath. David, with his pen still on the paper, looked up eagerly at his brother, participating in his feelings. A sigh which burst from Janet's bosom broke the silence.

'Ye maun go my bairn, as it seems to me that the Lord in His goodness points out the way. We will ask Him to guide and direct us. Ye should not go forth into the world without feeling sure that ye are under His protection, and that He will gie ye, my bairn, if ye ask Him with faith.'

'I know He will, and may be it was He who sent Mr Todd on to the links this afternoon to meet with me,' answered Donald, who, in his eagerness, was perfectly ready to agree with Janet.

'He orders the steps aright of all who serve Him,' observed Janet.

'Janet speaks the truth,' said David firmly. 'I wish that I could go with you.'

'Na! na! my bairn, you are not old eno' or hardy eno' to bear the rough life which Donald will ha' to lead in that strange country,' exclaimed Janet, who was not prepared to lose both of her boys at once. 'And oh, it is that terrible sea you will ha' to cross which troubles me to think of. Is there no other way of getting there?'

'I should be sorry if there was, for I have often

longed to sail over the ocean, and I look forward to the voyage with delight,' answered Donald. 'You must not think of the danger. Nothing worth having is to be gained without that, in my opinion, and we shall be having you safe on the other side of the ocean before long, I hope, Janet.'

'Na, na, my bairn, you maun come back to me, but that terrible ocean I could ne'er cross.'

'Donald no longer pressed that matter, and was content with the full permission Janet gave him to accept Mr Todd's offer, provided Margaret, on her return home, did not object. The young lady soon arrived, and, to Janet's surprise, entered at once warmly into Donald's projects.

That evening, as the family knelt down in prayer, Janet earnestly lifted up her voice in a petition that her bairn might be directed aright, and protected amid the dangers to which he would be exposed.

The next day, before returning to Mr Todd, Donald consulted his kind master, who advised him to accept the offer, and put him in the way of obtaining the instruction he required.

Janet, who had never allowed her charge to discover the means she employed for obtaining their support, told him to set his mind at rest about his outfit, which it had naturally occurred to him he should have a difficulty in obtaining. She at once went to Mr M'Tavish, who had continued her firm friend. 'An excellent opening for the lad,' he answered. 'I should be glad to help him, and let him come and shake me by the hand before he starts.'

Margaret, who besides obtaining many other female accomplishments from Mrs Galbraith, had learned to use her needle, had ample employment in manufacturing various articles of dress from the cloth Janet from time to time brought home with her. Mrs Galbraith, knowing how she was occupied, begged her to return home each day at an early hour that she might assist Janet, assuring her that she could readily spare her services. How eagerly Janet and Margaret sat and stitched away, allowing themselves but a short time for meals. They were determined to save expense, by making all Donald's underclothing themselves. Mr M'Tavish had desired Janet to let him order what outer clothing he required at the tailors, with a promise that he would see to the payment.

Donald meantime attended assiduously to his studies to prepare himself for the work he was expected to perform, so that he was longer absent from home than usual every day. His studies were congenial to his taste, and he entered into them with the more zeal that they were preparing him for the real work of life in which he had so long wished to engage.

David was always studious; and now that he had less of Donald's society, who was apt, when he could, to entice him out to join in the sports in which he himself delighted, he had more time than ever to attend to his books. Janet's great wish was that he should enter the ministry, but she had not yet broached the subject to him. Observing, however, his habits, she had little doubt that he would willingly agree to her proposal whenever she might make it.

'Surely the minister would like to have one of his bairns to follow in his footsteps,' she said to herself, 'and though it may cost more siller to prepare him for the work, I pray that what is needful may be supplied, and my old fingers will na' fail me for many a year to come.'

The time was approaching for Donald to take his departure. Margaret would have preferred consequently, as she had lately done, remaining with Janet, but her kind friend, Mrs Galbraith, was ill, and much required her services. Had Alec been at home, it is possible that she might not have thought it wise to have had so attractive a girl constantly with her, but Alec had been now for upwards of a year absent.

He had obtained, through his father's interest, a good situation in a mercantile house in London, and had latterly passed several months in Germany, where he had been sent on business with one of the

partners of the firm. He frequently wrote home,
giving a full account of himself and his proceedings,
as well as of the thoughts which occupied his mind.
Of late Mrs Galbraith had not been so well satisfied
as formerly with the tenor of his letters. His mind,
she was afraid, had become tinctured with that
German philosophy which is so sadly opposed to
all true spiritual religion. Mr Galbraith, who was
inclined to admire his son's sayings and doings,
told her not to fash herself on the subject, and that
he had no doubt Alec would remain faithful to the
kirk, though at his age it was but natural, mixing
in the world, that he should indulge in a few
fancies not in accordance with her notions. The
answer did not satisfy the wise and affectionate
mother.

'Such fancies ruin souls,' she observed. 'While
indulging in them he may be called hence without faith and hope, what then must his fate
be ?'

She wrote an earnest letter to Alec. The reply
was in his usual affectionate style ; but the part
touching the matter she considered of most import-
ance, was as utterly beyond her comprehension as
she suspected it was beyond that of the writer,
lucid as he apparently considered it. The replies
to several letters she wrote in succession, left matters
much as they were at first, and she could only pray
and look forward to his return, when she trusted

that her tender exhortations would produce a beneficial effect upon his mind.

'When he comes I must part with dear Margaret,' she said to herself. 'It will not do to have the two together. Alec may possibly attempt to impress his opinions on her mind, and may unsettle it should he fail to do more permanent injury; or, even should he keep them to himself, her sweet disposition, and other attractive qualities, may win his heart, while she may give her's in return, and I am sure that his father would never consent to his marrying a penniless orphan, and blame me for throwing them together.'

These thoughts, however, she kept within her own breast. Once entertained, they caused her much anxiety. While, on the one hand, she earnestly wished to have Alec home that she might speak to him personally; on the other, as her eyes fell on Margaret's sweet face, she feared the effect that face might have on her son. She must let her remain with Janet, that was settled; but Alec was sure to find his way to Janet's humble abode, as he had been accustomed to do when a boy to visit his schoolfellows, and he was very likely to suspect the cause of Margaret's absence from his mother's house.

Had she been able to look into the hearts of the young people, Mrs Galbraith would have had considerable cause for anxiety on the score of their meeting. Alec had had for many a day what might have been considered a boyish fancy for Margaret, while she regarded him as a brave, generous youth, who had saved her life, and her brother's best friend ; and though she had never examined her own feelings, she would have acknowledged that she considered him superior to any one else in the world.

Mr Galbraith, who never having for a moment thought about the subject, had no reason for speaking cautiously, came into the room one day while Margaret was seated with his wife, and exclaimed—

'Alec writes word that he wishes if possible to come home and see us, as he has had a fine offer made him which I have advised him to accept, and which will keep him away from England for some years. He is doubtful, however, whether he will be allowed time to come home, and if not we must console ourselves with the thoughts of his bright prospects. I should have been glad if you could have had a glimpse of him, but I purpose myself going up to London to see him off.'

'Oh, do try and get him to come home, if only for a few days,' exclaimed Mrs Galbraith. 'I could not bear the thoughts of his going away without seeing him. But you have not said where he is going ?'

'I will tell him to come if he can,' said Mr

Galbraith, 'he is not, however, going to a distant country, but merely to Canada, where he is to assist in forming a branch of the firm, either at Montreal or Toronto, as the partners are anxious to commence without delay. I consider the appointment a feather in the cap of so young a man.'

Margaret listened eagerly to all that was said. She was very certain that Alec was fitted for any post which might be assigned to him. She trusted, however, he would find time to get home and see them.

'Donald and he will meet to a certainty; how delightful for both of them, and we shall hear from each how the other is getting on, and they will be of mutual assistance. Perhaps they will go out in the same ship,' she thought.

Both Mrs Galbraith and Margaret were to be disappointed. A letter was received from Alec two days later, saying that the vessel which was to convey Mr Elliott, the principal of the firm, and himself, was to sail immediately, and that no time could be allowed him to run down to Scotland. Mrs Galbraith greatly felt this announcement, but this was not the chief cause of her sorrow. She had long felt her health failing, and knowing that her days were numbered, she feared that she should never again see her son. All she could do was to commend him to the protecting care of Heaven, and to pray, from the very depths of her soul, that even

though it might be through trials and troubles, he
might be brought to accept the truth as it is in
Christ Jesus, and have a living faith in His all
sufficient sacrifice. Would that all mothers prayed
thus for their absent sons exposed to the wiles of
Satan and the snares and temptations of the world.
Such prayers would assuredly be heard ; how many
wandering sheep would be brought into the fold of
Christ ?

Margaret felt very sad when she heard that
Alec was not coming, but she kept her feelings to
her own bosom. She had to return home to assist
Janet in completing Donald's outfit. She and her
old nurse worked harder than ever, there still
seemed so much to be done, and Mr Todd had
sent Donald word that he must hold himself in
readiness to start at a short notice. The expected
order came.

'Fare-ye-weel my bairn, fare-ye-weel, ne'er
forget that the deil, like a roaring lion, is ganging
about to seek whom he may devour, and put your
trust in Him who is able and willing to save you
out of all your troubles. They maun come ; dinna
fancy all is sunshine in the world, but He will be
your shield and buckler in time of danger if you
love and serve Him.'

Janet, as she spoke, threw her arms round
Donald's neck, and big tears dropped from her eyes.
Margaret clung to him, and kissed his cheek again

and again, till he had to tear himself away ; when accompanied by David, he went on board the vessel which was to convey him to Leith, whence he was to proceed on to London. David remained with him till the last, and then returned to Janet's humble abode to apply himself to his books.

CHAPTER V.

Donald's voyage to Canada.—He gains the friendship of Mr Skinner.—Reaches Quebec.—Voyage up the St Lawrence. —Arrival at the new township.—Description of the settlement.—Mr Skinner preaches the gospel, and takes up his residence in the place.

ONALD found himself in a new world on board the fine emigrant ship, which was conveying him and nearly three hundred settlers to Canada. They were of every rank, calling, and character, but one object seemed to animate them all—an eager desire to establish themselves and obtain wealth in the new country to which they were bound. Some talked loudly of the honour and glory of subduing the wilderness, and creating an inheritance for their children ; though among them Donald observed many whom he was sure would never do either the one or the other.

Though frank and open-hearted, influenced by the usual caution of a Scotchman, Donald did not feel disposed to form friendships with any of his fellow-passengers until he had ascertained their characters. His time, indeed, was fully occupied in pursuing the professional studies he had com-

60

menced at home, and in doing work for Mr Todd. There was one person on board, however, who excited his interest. He was a man of middle age, and of mild and quiet manners, while the expression of his eyes and mouth betokened firmness and determination. Donald could hear nothing about him except that his name was Skinner, and that he was not connected with any of the parties of settlers on board. His conversation showed an enlightened mind, but he seemed at first rather inclined to obtain information than to impart it. Perhaps he also wished to gain an insight into the characters of his companions before he allowed of any intimacy. Wherever he was, however, he would allow of no light or frivolous conversation, and he did not hesitate to rebuke those who gave utterance to any profane or coarse expressions. Donald had heard him spoken of as an over religious man. That he was a strict one he had evidence, when one day, while several fellow-voyagers were indulging in unseemly conversation, Mr Skinner approached them.

'Will you allow me to ask you a question, and I trust you will not be offended, are you Christians?' he asked.

'Of course, Mr Skinner, of course we are,' answered two or three of the party, in the same breath.

'Then you will desire to follow the example of the Master whose name you bear,' he replied.

'And He has said, "Be ye holy for I am holy." "By their fruits shall ye know them." Now the fruits of the lips which you have been producing are directly opposed to His commands. Can you suppose that He who hears all you utter will be otherwise than grieved and offended with the words you have just been speaking? Out of the mouth the heart speaketh. Let me entreat you to examine your hearts, and judge what is within them, and then ask yourselves whether they have been changed. Whether "you are holy as God is holy," whether you are real or only nominal Christians. You are voyaging together to a country where you expect to prosper—to secure an independence, and to enjoy happiness and contentment for the remainder of your lives; but, my friends, would you not act wisely to look beyond all this? As our voyage in this ship must come to an end, so must our voyage through life, and what then? Again I repeat, that though by nature depraved, prone to evil, full of sin, with hearts desperately wicked, God says to all who desire to enter the kingdom of heaven, to become heirs of eternal life, to be prepared to go and dwell with Him, to enjoy eternal happiness instead of eternal misery, "Be ye holy as I am holy." You will ask me, how can that be? I reply, take God at His word. He would not tell us to be what we cannot be. He does not mock us with His commands. He has said, "Believe in the Lord Jesus

Christ and thou shalt be saved." But He does not
mean that your belief is to be merely affirmative;
it is not sufficient only to acknowledge that Christ
lived and died on the cross. All Scripture shows
that you must have a living active faith in the com-
plete and finished work of Christ. You must look
to Him as *your* Saviour; you must know that His
blood was shed for *you individually*, and acknowledge His great love for you, which brought Him
down from the glories of heaven to suffer on the
cross, and that love must create a love in your hearts,
and make you desirous of imitating Him and serving
Him. You must turn from your sins and strive to
hate sin, and in this you will have the all-sufficient
aid of His Holy Spirit. Thus, though as I have
said, in yourselves unrighteous, sinful, impure and
doing things that you would not, yet, washed in the
blood of Jesus, God no longer looks on your iniqui-
ties. He blots your sins out of remembrance. He
puts them away as far as the east is from the west
He imputes Christ's righteousness to you. He
clothes you in Christ's pure and spotless garments.
He declares you to be " holy as He is holy."'

Some of the young men he addressed hung down
their heads, and others tried to make their escape,
but two or three fixed their eyes earnestly on the
speaker, whose manner was so kind and gentle that
none could be offended, however little they might
have been disposed to agree with the doctrine he

enunciated. Among the latter was Donald Morrison. He had heard many excellent sermons; he had listened respectfully to the religious instruction which Janet, according to the light within her, attempted to give him, but he had seldom heard the truth so plainly and earnestly put before him, or at all events he had never so clearly comprehended it.

Finding several of the party inclined to listen, Mr Skinner continued his address, urging his hearers at once to accept the merciful offers of salvation so freely made. As is generally the case where the gospel is preached, some were inclined to side with the preacher, while others were stirred by the natural depravity of the human heart, instigated by Satan to more determined opposition.

Donald was induced from what he heard to examine his own heart. He had not before been aware that it was depraved by nature and prone to evil; that it must be renewed before he could love and truly serve Christ. He had been trusting to his own good principles, to his desire to do right; and he had been prepared to go forward and fight the battle of life, relying on his own strength. Happy are those who make the important discovery he did before the strife commences, before temptation comes in their way, or an overthrow, often a fatal one, is certain. Donald had believed that by living morally and honestly, and by labouring hard, he should merit admission to that heaven where Christ would reign as king ; but he had never truly comprehended the necessity of the atonement—that sins must remain registered against the sinner unless washed away by the blood of Jesus, and that His blood can alone be applied through the simple faith of the sinner.

From that day forward Donald sought every opportunity of conversing with Mr Skinner, who was never weary of answering his questions and solving his doubts. Mr Todd expressed some fears that his young friend would become so engrossed with religious subjects, that he would neglect his professional duties, and yet Mr Todd held religion in great respect, and believed that he made the Bible his guide in life.

'I am very sure, my dear sir, that no man who truly loves and obeys the Saviour will, in consequence, become a worse citizen, or be less attentive to his worldly duties,' answered Mr Skinner, to whom the remark was made. 'And I trust you will find Donald Morrison no exception to the rule.'

Donald spent a portion of each day with Mr Skinner, sometimes reading with him, at others walking the deck, as the ship glided smoothly over the ocean.

Their passage was somewhat long, for calms prevailed, but it was prosperous, and at length the emigrant ship entered the waters of the magnificent St Lawrence, and finally came to an anchor before

E

the renowned city of Quebec, which looked down
smiling on the voyagers from its rocky heights.

There was eager hurry and bustle on board, for
the emigrants were anxious to land, while on shore
a general activity prevailed, as it was the busy time
of the year, when merchantmen, long barred by the
ice which bound up the river during winter, were
daily arriving, and the huge timber ships were
receiving their cargoes of logs, brought down
through innumerable streams and lakes which in-
tersect the country, hundreds of miles from the
far-off interior.

The emigrants now separated, some to go to the
eastern townships or other parts of the Lower Pro-
vince, but the greater number to proceed up the
St Lawrence, and across Lake Ontario to the magnificent district then being opened up, bounded west
and south by Lakes Ontario, St Clare, and Erie.

Donald found, to his satisfaction, that Mr Skinner was going in the same direction.   Donald knew
no more than at first who Mr Skinner was ; he was
satisfied, however, that he was a true man, with a
single eye to God's service.

'I may possibly settle among you,' said his new
friend.   'Wherever human beings are collected together, there I find my work.'

'Are you a minister then?' asked Donald.

'Are not all Christ's faithful servants His minis-
ters?' asked Mr Skinner, 'called on by Him to

make known His great love to perishing sinners;
to tell them the only way by which they can be
saved? In that sense I reply yes to your question.
My young friend I desire not to eat the bread of
idleness, nor to take aught from other men's
hands.'

Donald felt that he ought not to press his question further.

The party ascended the river in a sailing vessel
to Montreal, and from thence Kingston was reached
by stage waggons, which conveyed them along the
banks of the river where the navigation was im-
peded by rapids, though the greater part of the
journey was performed in large boats up the St
Lawrence and through the beautiful lake of the
'Thousand Islands.'

'I wish Margaret and David could have a sight
of this lovely scenery,' said Donald to his friend, as
they glided by numberless islets in succession, covered with rich and varied foliage.

'Their steps may some day be directed hither,'
answered Mr Skinner, who was even a warmer
admirer of the beauties of nature than his young
companion.

At Kingston they embarked on board a large
schooner. Next morning, when Donald came on
deck, his surprise was great to find the vessel out of
sight of land. The water was perfectly smooth; a
thin mist hung over it, which probably concealed

the nearer northern shore, for as the sun rose, he could distinguish in that direction a long low line of coast, fringed with the trees of the primeval forest. Here and there, as they sailed along, small openings could be perceived, where settlements had lately been formed, and the giants of the forest had fallen beneath the woodman's axe.

The voyage terminated at Toronto, till lately called Little York, on the western shore of the lake, but a long journey had yet to be performed across the peninsula to the district Mr Todd had undertaken to settle. Waggons and drays were put in requisition to convey the party and their goods through the forest, while the leader and his staff, with other gentlemen, rode on ahead to prepare for their reception. Donald wondered how vehicles with wheels could make their way amid the stumps of trees, along the track which then formed the only road to the settlement. Here and there were swamps, which were made passable by huge trunks of trees laid across the track, and bridges of timber, of a primitive, though of a strong character, had already been thrown across the streams.

'You see pioneers have been before us,' observed Mr Todd to Donald. 'Settlers direct from the old country would have been appalled with the difficulties the well-trained backwoodsmen have overcome.'

Here and there were small clearings, in the

centre of which log houses had been put up, to serve as wayside inns. At one of these Mr Todd and his party halted as evening closed in. The accommodation was scanty, though an ample meal of eggs and bacon and corn cakes, was served on a long table which stood in the middle of the public room. Upon it, beneath, and on the benches at the sides, the guests, wrapped in their cloaks, with their saddles for pillows, passed the night. Donald, before lying down, went out to take a turn in front of the hut. As he looked along the cutting towards the west, a bright glare met his eyes. It at once struck him that the forest must be on fire, and he was hastening back to warn his companions, when he met Mr Skinner.

'There is no danger,' observed the latter. 'We will proceed along the road, and you will see the cause.'

The light from the fire enabled them to find their way among the stumps, and they soon saw before them an opening in the forest, in the centre of which blazed a huge pile of vast trunks of trees, surrounded by men, who, with long pitchforks, were throwing faggots under the trunks to assist in consuming them.

'Although these trees would be worth many pounds by the water-edge, here they are valueless and in the way, and no other mode has been discovered of disposing of them,' observed Mr Skinner to Donald. 'Yet I always regret to see the destruction of those magnificent productions with which God has clothed the earth, but thousands and tens of thousands of those monarchs of the forest are destined ere long to fall to make way for the habitation of man. Yet one living soul is of more value than them all, and we may hope that many a voice may be raised to Him in hymns of praise amid this region, hitherto a wilderness, and which has resounded only with the howl of the savage wolf, or the fierce war songs of the long benighted inhabitants of the land.'

A busy scene presented itself as the cavalcade at length reached the new settlement. Here and there, amid the stumps of trees, were scattered tents, shanties, and log-huts, either finished or in the course of erection. Women were cooking over fires in front of their rude dwellings, while their children played around. Oxen, urged on by the cries of their drivers, were dragging up huge logs to form the walls of the huts. Drays were conveying sawn timber from the banks of the broad stream which flowed by on one side—a saw-mill, turned by its water, being already busily at work. A little way off, the tall trees were falling with loud crashes before the woodmen's axes, engaged in enlarging the borders of the settlement. While here and there arose edifices of greater pretensions than their neighbours, with weather-boarded sides and roofs.

Several broad roads intersected the projected town at right angles, from which, however, no attempt had as yet been made to remove the stumps of the trees; while all around arose the dark wall formed by the forest, closely hemming in the clearing, with the exception of the single opening through which the travellers had made their way.

'This is a wild place, indeed,' said Donald, as he surveyed the scene.

'It was wilder a few months ago,' answered Mr Todd. 'It is our task to reduce it into order, and ere long we shall see handsome houses, gaily painted cottages, blooming orchards, green pastures, and fields waving with rich corn, in lieu of the scene which now meets our eyes. But we have no time to lose. We must select a spot by the river for the new settlers to camp on, obtain a supply of wood for their fires, and get some shanties put up for the women and children and old people.'

Mr Todd and his attendants dismounted at the door of the chief inn. It was also a store, at which every iron article, from a plough to a needle, all sorts of haberdashery and clothing, groceries, stationery, drugs and beer, wines and spirits, could be procured, as the proprietor, who shook hands with the new arrivals, informed them.

Donald was soon actively engaged under Mr Todd in the duties of his office, and from that day forward till the close of the summer he had very

few minutes he could call his own, with the exception of those granted during the blessed day of rest.
He now learned to value the Sabbath more than
ever, when he could rest from the toils of the week,
and leave his surveying staff and chains, his axe
and note-book, and turn with earnest faith to God's
Word. No chapel or church had as yet arisen,
and the gospel would not have been proclaimed
had not Mr Skinner invited the inhabitants to meet
him beneath the shade of the lofty trees, where,
with his own hands, he had cleared away the brush-
wood. Here he proclaimed the glad tidings of salvation by the blood of the Lamb, to many who had
never before heard the glorious news. Many as-
sembled gladly, especially the settlers from bonnie
Scotland ; some came from curiosity, or to pass
away the time ; and a few to mock at the un-
authorized preacher, who, in his ordinary dress,
ventured, as they asserted, to set himself up among
his fellows. Provided souls were won, the stranger
cared nothing for the remarks which might be
made.

He had purchased a plot of ground on the banks
of the stream, some way removed from the township,
and here, with the aid of three or four hired labour-
ers, he had made a clearing and erected a log-hut,
at which Donald was always a welcome guest, with
several others who came to hear God's Word ex-
plained.

The winter came on, and snow covered the ground, but the axemen went on with their labours, and the tall trunks they felled could now with greater ease be dragged either to the saw-mill, to the spots where log-huts were to be erected, to form snake fencing, or to the great heaps prepared for burning. Donald was surprised to find how rapidly the months went by, and how soon the period of the year at which he had arrived in Canada had returned.

CHAPTER VI.

Letters from home.—Margaret loses her friend.—Unsatisfactory report of Alec.—David resolves to go out.—Donald urges his sister and Janet to come also, and prepares for their reception.—No tidings can be obtained of Alec.—David's arrival.—Mr Skinner explains to him important gospel truths.

DONALD had frequently written home, and had heard from Margaret and David in return. Every word from them was of interest to him, and all kind Janet's sayings and doings were faithfully recorded. She seemed to work even harder than ever; but as Margaret remarked :—

'She manages to make her purchases at a cheapness that surprises me, and I often cannot account for the number of articles she brings home for the money she has to expend. Perhaps she gets more for her yarn than formerly, or has a hoard with which we are unacquainted. Mrs Galbraith is as kind as ever, and gives me a number of things which assist me greatly. Her health is, I fear,

74

however, failing rapidly, and if she is taken away
I shall lose the best friend I ever expect to have,
next to Janet. She hears occasionally from Alec,
who is at Montreal, which is, I suppose, a long way
from you, or you would have mentioned him. Mr
Galbraith has much altered; he looks grave and
anxious, and is often irritable with his dear wife.
I pray that she may be spared, but I am very
very anxious about her.'

The next letter to this acknowledged with pleasure and gratitude the receipt of the first sum of
money Donald was able to send home. Margaret
wrote:—'It has made us rich beyond our most
sanguine hope ; but Janet seems unwilling to spend
any of it, and says she does not like to deprive you
of your siller ; so pray do not send any more unless
we really require it. Mrs Galbraith is kinder than
ever, and insists on giving me everything I can
possibly want, saying that I am of so much service
to her that I ought to receive a salary in addition.
I, of course, only do what I can to show my gratitude for her kindness to me since I was a little
girl.'

Another letter came from Margaret some months
after this, when Donald had been in the colony upwards of a couple of years. Her kind friend, Mrs
Galbraith, had been taken away, and though she
had died with the hope that Alec would be brought
to know the truth, she had been for the last few

months of her life so deeply anxious about his
spiritual welfare, that she could not help speaking
on the subject to Margaret, who had hitherto not
been aware of the dangerous notions he had im-
bibed. Margaret expressed herself deeply grieved
with what she heard, and promised to unite her
prayers with those of her friend for Alec's conversion.

A few months later Donald again heard from
Margaret. Mr Galbraith had followed his wife to
the grave. Her exhortations to him had not been
in vain, and having accepted the truth himself, he
was as anxious about his son as she had been. 'I
visited him frequently during his illness, as Mrs
Galbraith had entreated me to do,' said Margaret,
'and though he was undoubtedly most anxious about
Alec's spiritual state, he also, from what he said,
seemed to fear that his worldly prospects were very
different from what he had hoped. The mercantile
house with which he is connected has failed, and I
fear that the greater part—if not all—of Mr Galbraith's property has been lost also, so that Alec
will be left without support unless he can obtain
another situation. I need not suggest to you, my
dear brother, to write to your old friend, and ascertain his position, and if he requires it give him a
helping hand. I must now tell you the determination to which David has come, though he will write
to you himself on the subject. We were not till

lately aware of the assistance we have received from dear Mrs Galbraith and other friends, from whom we have discovered our kind Janet has been in the habit of demanding whatever she considered necessary for us. I am sure that she would not have begged a sixpence for her own support. I am now thrown more completely than ever on her hands, and though I am anxious to do anything I can to maintain myself she will not hear of my leaving her. I would take a situation as a child's governess, or as a companion to a lady, such as I have been to Mrs Galbraith, or go into service, but she insists that I must bide at home with her, as she could not trust me out of her sight, but that I am welcome to ply my needle as much as I please, and that she doubts not she shall find work for me if I follow her wishes, which David is anxious that I should do. He cannot bring himself to draw on her resources, so as to continue his studies till he can become a minister, which will not be for some years yet. He has often talked of going out to join you in Canada, and his heart is, I am sure, set on so doing. He has his doubts as to his fitness for the ministry, and says that head-learning and book-learning are not sufficient, and that he is conscious of being destitute of all other qualifications. He declares he should sink down with nervousness directly he enters a pulpit, that his voice and memory would fail him, and that he does not possess that love of souls and desire to win them to Christ, which he considers the chief qualification for the preacher of the gospel. I agreed with him when he made the last remark; but still I trust that he is mistaken about his qualifications. Nothing I have urged has had any effect in inducing him to alter his determination. Though he studies as hard as ever, he almost starves himself in his anxiety not to be a burden to Janet, he will not buy any fresh books, or spend more money than he can possibly help; indeed, I must own to you that she would have great difficulty in giving him any, though she tries to make him believe, as usual, that she has as much as he can require. I begged you before not to send us home any of your earnings; but I do not hesitate now to ask you to remit as much as will be sufficient for David's voyage, if you approve of his going out to join you.'

'The very thing of all others I have been longing for,' exclaimed Donald, as he finished Margaret's letter. 'I have ample to enable him to come out, and I am sure Mr Todd will find employment for him. But Margaret and Janet must not remain with straitened means; I wish they would come out also. I will send home sufficient for their voyage, and use every argument to induce them to come. If they will not they must spend the money on their own support at home. Margaret will, I am sure, be perfectly happy out here, though Janet would find the country rather strange, yet neither of them would mind the rough life they would be compelled to live, any more than others do, many of whom have been far more accustomed than they are to the luxuries and refinements of the old country.'

Thus Donald meditated till he persuaded himself that in a few months he should see his sister and brother and their faithful nurse arrive to take possession of the log hut he proposed building for them. He lost no time in writing a letter, and in arranging with Mr Todd to send home a considerable portion of the salary due to him. He insisted that Margaret should receive whatever David did not require for his passage-money and journey to the township, and should spend it on the support of Janet and herself, should they decline accompanying David. He thought it impossible that they could refuse, and forthwith set to work to build a substantial log hut on a plot of ground which, by Mr Todd's advice and assistance, he had purchased not far from Mr Skinner's location.

Mr Skinner had made inquiries about his family when he heard of his hopes of being joined by his brother and sister and old nurse. He at once begged that he would apply to him for whatever he might require for their comfort and convenience.

'I am a bachelor, and as my personal expenses are trifling, I shall consider it a privilege to be allowed to be of use to those who are so well deserving of assistance,' he observed. ' That old nurse of yours has excited my warm admiration. Her knowledge may be limited, but from your account she has lived a practical Christian life, and though you may justly desire to be independent, and to support yourself by your own labour, you cannot wish her and your sister to decline whatever aid God puts it into the hearts of others to offer to them.'

Donald warmly thanked his friend; and seeing the justness of his remarks, without hesitation accepted his offer. His mind was thereby greatly relieved from any anxiety he might have felt in supporting those who had become dependent upon him, till he himself should be able to gain sufficient for the purpose.

He wrote immediately to Alec Galbraith, but some time passed, and no answer was received to his letter. He then got Mr Todd to make inquiries of some acquaintances at Montreal, and through them he at last heard that after the house in which Alec had been engaged had broken up, the young man having vainly attempted to find employment in other firms, had left the place without letting anyone know in what direction he had gone. He had created many enemies by the opinions he publicly expressed on religious and political subjects, and was looked upon as a disloyal and dangerous person.

This account greatly grieved Donald, who had not supposed it possible that the fine manly and talented friend of his youth would be otherwise than liked, and succeed wherever he might go. 'What can possibly have changed Alec so much?' he asked himself more than once.

Donald mentioned the subject to Mr Skinner.

'What was the foundation of his good qualities?' inquired his friend. 'Were they built on the rock which, when the floods of trial and temptation came would stand firm, or on the sandy soil, whence they were sure to be washed away.'

Donald considered. 'He resided in Germany for some time, and I know that his religious opinions underwent a change for the worse, and from some remarks Margaret let drop, that his mother was very anxious about him.'

'That is a sufficient explanation,' observed Mr Skinner, with a sigh. 'We must pray that like the prodigal son he may find that he has husks alone to eat, and be brought back to the loving Father, who, with open arms, is ever ready to receive those who, having made that important discovery, return to Him.'

The two Christian friends knelt down and offered up their petitions that the wanderer might be found out and restored.

Few people in the settlement were more busy than Donald Morrison. Besides building his log house, at which he worked with his own hands, and superintending the clearing of the ground, he had his official duties to attend to, which he in no way neglected; and, as the settlement increased, they became more onerous than at first. 'If David were with me he would find plenty to do,' he said, over and over again. 'I wish that he were coming, and I have no doubt Mr Todd would obtain for him a situation under me.'

When Donald wrote home he had begged his brother and sister not to wait till they could write and announce their intended coming, but if they could persuade Janet to accompany them, to set off immediately. As each party of settlers arrived he looked out eagerly, hoping to find those so dear to him among them. He was destined frequently to be disappointed.

At last, one evening he was seated in his new house, now nearly completed, busily employed on some plans which he had taken home from Mr Todd's office, when he was aroused by a knock at the door. On opening it he saw standing before him a tall slight young man, whom he knew by his bonnet and tartan coat to be Scotch. 'Does one Donald Morrison live here?' asked the stranger, gazing eagerly at his face. The moment he spoke Donald knew the voice; it was David's, and the brothers' hands were clasped together.

'I should not have known you,' exclaimed

David, scanning Donald's sunburnt countenance, and sturdy strongly built figure.

'Nor I you, till I heard you speak,' answered Donald. 'But have you not brought Margaret and Janet?'

'I am sorry to say no. Janet would not venture across the salt ocean, and Margaret would not quit her. Janet, indeed, did her utmost to dissuade me from coming to this land of impenetrable forests, fierce red men, savage wolves, roaring cataracts, and numberless other dangers, such as she believes it is, and her dread of exposing Margaret to them, I suspect, made her more determined to stay at home than had she herself alone been asked to come, as for our sakes I believe she would have risked all could she have been satisfied that Margaret would have been in safety. Finding all my arguments useless, I set off as you wished me.'

'She is a good faithful creature, and we must still hope to overcome her fears for our dear sister's safety,' said Donald. 'However, I am thankful you have come, and I am sure that you will not be disappointed.'

Donald lost no time in placing an abundant supply of bachelor's fare, prepared by his own hands, on the table. As may be supposed, the brothers sat up the greater part of the night, talking over the past as well as their future prospects.

Donald was not disappointed in his hopes of

obtaining employment for David, Mr Todd being glad at once, on his brother's recommendation, to secure his services. David gave his mind to the work he had undertaken, and soon became a very efficient assistant to Donald. Though he looked pale and delicate when he first arrived, and was unable to go through the physical exertion required of him without fatigue, he rapidly gained strength, and in a short time became strong and hardy.

Shortly after his arrival Donald took him to call on Mr Skinner, who welcomed him kindly, and led him to enter freely into conversation, that he might, as Donald suspected, ascertain his opinions. Donald, when speaking of his brother, had merely stated that he declined entering the ministry, and preferred coming out to join him as a settler. Mr Skinner allowed several days to pass, during which they frequently met, before he offered any remarks to David on the choice he had made.

'You have abandoned the most important of callings, my young friend, for one which, though honourable and useful, and which may obtain to you worldly advantages, is not, in the nature of things, likely to render spiritual service to your fellow creatures, he observed.

'Several reasons prompted me to take the course I have pursued,' answered David. 'The principle one, however, was, that I felt myself unfitted for the ministry, and had a strong desire to come out and join my brother. I had no spiritual life in myself, and could not impart it to others.'

'Certainly you could not impart to others what you did not possess yourself,' observed Mr Skinner. 'But, my dear friend, are you content to remain without that spiritual life? It is required, not only for those engaged in the ministry, but for all who rightly bear the name of Christ, for all who desire to be His subjects, to enter into the kingdom of heaven. The Holy Spirit alone can impart it to you or to others, but having it, whether set apart or not for Christ's service, you may be made the instrument by which many of your fellow-creatures may obtain it likewise. It should be the object of all Christ's subjects to win souls for Him. When Christ spoke to Nicodemus and told him that he must be born again, He addressed a learned man, an expounder of the law of Moses. If a physician, a merchant, or person of any other calling, had come to Him He would have said the same. And now I entreat you to ask yourself the question, which Christ would have put had you gone to Him. He would have said, as He said to Nicodemus, 'Ye must be born again.' He would not have first inquired whether or not you were intended for the ministry. He would have said, as He does to all human beings, high and low, rich and poor, men and women, boys and girls, who desire to live with Him in heaven for ever and ever. You may be very in-

dustrious, and energetic, and honest, and moral, and
well conducted in your secular calling, but that will
not stand you instead of what Christ requires.
The old man must be put off, the new nature be
received. I repeat, ' You must be born again.'

' And how can that be brought about?' exclaimed
Donald, much perturbed in mind.

' Christ says, " the wind bloweth where it listeth,
and thou hearest the sound thereof, but canst not
tell whence it cometh and whither it goeth, so is
everyone that is born of the Spirit." Christ did
not leave Nicodemus with this answer, which might
well have perplexed him, as it has those who have
turned aside from it as incomprehensible ; but He
shows how man must do his part to bring about
that new birth. It is by *simple faith, by taking God
at His word*, by looking to Christ and trusting to
His blood as all-sufficient to wash away sin, to His
sacrifice as being accepted in lieu of our punishment.
He explains it in those most blessed words—that
most perfect of all similes—" As Moses lifted up
the serpent in the wilderness, even so must the Son
of man be lifted up, that whosoever believeth in
Him should not perish but have eternal life." Know
and feel that you are bitten by sin, dying eternally
from its rank poison, and then look to Jesus as the
certain, the only cure, just as the Israelites, bitten by
the fiery serpents, were commanded to look at the
brazen serpent, held up by Moses in the wilder-

ness, as the only way by which they could be cured. Thus, through simple faith, is the necessary change brought about. All God demands from us is faith. He, through the Holy Spirit, does the rest. My dear young friend read that all-important portion of God's Word with earnest prayer for enlightenment, and you will understand the simple plan of salvation, which His loving mercy has formed, far more clearly than you can by any words I may use. The question is, Do you believe that the Bible is God's Word, that Jesus Christ, His Son, came into the world to suffer, the just for the unjust—that the world, through Him, might be saved? If you do, then hear His words,—'He that believeth on me is not condemned.' If you do believe, then you are born again, for all who are not born again remain under condemnation. What you require, what we all require, is more grace, more faith, more love, more trust. For all those things we can pray, and wrestle, and strive, and God will not allow us to pray in vain. Faith may be a strong rope or a thin rope, so thin that we dread its giving way ; but God *forms* it, *God holds it fast*. In His hands it will not break. Let us then trust in Him, and ever seek the aid of the Holy Spirit to hold us up, and we shall find the thin line increasing in size till it becomes a stout cable, capable of, aye certain of, holding our wave-tossed bark amid the fiercest tempest which can break around us.

David returned home rejoicing. He did not regret abandoning his former intention and coming out to Canada; but he resolved to give himself up to the study of the Bible, and while following his secular calling, to assist his friend in spreading the truths of the gospel among the surrounding population.

CHAPTER VII.

Donald's expedition through the forest.—Attacked by wolves.—
Relieved from them by a hurricane, and narrowly escapes
being crushed by falling trees.

ONALD having David now to attend to
his office work, frequently made expeditions to long distances where it was proposed to establish fresh townships. These were
performed on foot, and he had become so expert a
backwood's man, that he had no hesitation in trusting himself without a guide. He, however, carried
his gun, and in summer a fishing rod, that he
might supply himself with provisions by the way.
His gun also he required for defence against any
wolves or bears he might encounter, both of which
were at that time common in the country, though
long since driven off to the wilder regions of the far
west and north.

He was returning from one of these expeditions
in the early spring, when night approaching, as he
was making his way through the forest, he prepared to encamp. His axe quickly enabled him to
cut some sticks for his shanty, for which a quantity
of large pieces of birch bark scattered about served

89

as a covering. The tops of some young spruce firs strewed on the ground made a luxurious couch, while there was no lack of dry broken branches to furnish a supply of firewood. He quickly formed his hunter's camp, and commenced cooking a couple of fish he had caught in a stream he had shortly before forded, and a bird he had shot during the day. This, with a handful of Indian meal made into porridge, gave him a sumptuous repast. After reading God's Word by the light of his blazing fire, he commended himself to His merciful care, and having renewed his fire, lay down within his hut fearless of danger.

His journey had been long and fatiguing, which made him sleep soundly. He was at length awakened by a long low howl. He opened his eyes and discovered that his fire had gone out, but he was still too much oppressed by sleep to rise. He was under the impression that he had merely dreamed of the noise he had heard. It shortly came again, however, and this time he was aware that it was a reality. Mixed with the howl were the sounds of savage barks and yelps. He knew them to be the voices of wolves, disputing, probably, over the body of some deer they had pulled down, or found dead after it had escaped from the hunter's rifle. Their repast finished, they might come in the direction of his camp. Starting up he prepared to relight his fire, and drawing the wood together, which he had kept for the purpose, he quickly produced a flame, and then looked to the priming of his gun to be ready in case of an attack. To sleep longer was out of the question ; he therefore sat up, listening to the appalling sounds which ever and anon echoed through the forest. He had hitherto in his journies never fallen in with a pack of wolves, though he had frequently met solitary individuals, whose savage jaws had shown what fearful foes, a number combined together, would prove. His stout Highland heart was not, however, inclined to give way to fear ; besides which, his faith was firm, and he knew in whom he trusted. At the same time, not being a mere enthusiast, he felt that it was his duty to consider what were the best means of preserving his life by his own exertions, should the wolves discover him, and venture on an attack. He first collected all the fuel he could find near at hand, and made his fire blaze up brightly. As, however, it might not last till the morning, it occurred to him that it would be wise to examine the neighbouring trees, and to select one up which he might climb, should the savage creatures come round him.

The larger trees were inaccessible ; but he found one near at hand, the lower branches of which he might reach, could he manage to drive a few pegs into the trunk. With his axe he at once cut some holes as high as he could reach, and then sharpening several pieces of wood, hardening them in the

fire. The trunk was soft, and to his satisfaction he
found that he could make a ladder, by which he
could reach the lowest branches, and thence gain a
part of the tree which would afford him a secure
seat, and enable him to fire down upon his assailants,
and, as he hoped, drive them away.

The night wind blowing keenly, he had no wish
to take his seat on the tree till compelled by necessity. Having therefore made his arrangements he
again threw fuel on the fire, and sat down within
the shelter of his hut, with his gun by his side.
The howling of the wolves had ceased, and he hoped
that they had turned away from him, and that he
should not be troubled by a visit. A feeling of
security stole over him, and fatigue overcoming his
prudence, he again dropped off to sleep.

How long he had thus sat with his eyes closed
he could not tell, when he was awakened by hearing
the savage howls of the wolves close to him. Starting up he caught sight of numberless dark forms,
with glaring eyes, making a circle round the fire,
which they were evidently unwilling to approach,
eager as they were to seize their prey. The fire had
burnt somewhat low, and he feared that should the
flames cease to ascend they might make a dash across
the embers, and rush upon him.

The tree he had selected was at hand, and he
now regretted that he had not ascended it at first.
A few dry sticks were still within his reach. Spring-

ing out of his hut he seized them, and threw them on the fire. At that moment a savage wolf, either one of the leaders of the pack, or more hungry than its companions, made a rush at him from one side. Happily he was prepared, and firing, the creature rolled over. The instant it was dead the rest of the animals sprang on the body, tearing it to pieces. Donald on this, after re-loading his gun, having stirred up the fire so as to make it burn more brightly, ran towards the tree, up which he began to climb. The short delay of loading his gun might have proved fatal, for part of the pack perceiving him, came yelping on furiously, and he had scarcely got his feet out of the reach of their fangs before the whole pack had collected round him. His gun, which he had slung at his back, being rather weighty, he was afraid that the pegs would give way, and that he should fall among the ravenous jaws below him, but he succeeded at length in reaching a firm branch, and he drew himself up on to it, and thence climbed to the point he had selected.

Here he sat securely. Though he had escaped from the wolves they showed no signs of quitting him ; the light of the fire, which still blazed up brightly, exhibiting their savage forms, as they stood howling beneath the tree, or circled round and round, looking up with eager eyes towards him. He refrained from firing, believing that they were more likely to go away when they found that they could not reach him, than if he should kill some of their number, when the pack would remain to devour the carcases of their companions. At last, when morning dawned, and they still continued round the tree, he began to lose patience, and to fear that they would carry on the siege till they had starved him out.

' I cannot kill the whole pack,' he said to himself, ' but I may knock over so many that the others may at length take warning and make their escape.'

He had no difficulty in firing, and as a branch offered him a good rest for his gun, he was able to take steady aim, and never missed a shot.

He had killed half a dozen or more, still the wolves continued round the tree. It was in a dense part of the forest, through which the beams of the sun did not penetrate, or the creatures, disliking the bright light of day, would probably have retreated to their fastness. Hour after hour passed by, the air became unusually sultry and hot, even in the forest. Donald was growing, at the same time, very hungry, and though, as yet, he had rather enjoyed the adventure, he now began to feel seriously anxious about his safety. He had but a few bullets remaining, and the small shot in his pouch would produce but little effect on the heads of the wolves, and only render them more savage. He waited for some time, and then again began to fire, hoping that the sound of his piece might be heard by any party of Indians or travellers in the forest, who would come to his assistance, for he knew that the wolves, cowardly though savage, will seldom venture to attack several people together. He had expended his bullets. He felt more and more sensible of the increased heat, and on looking upwards through the branches he observed an unusual appearance in the sky. The wolves, at the same instant, became silent, and then seized, so it seemed, by a panic, the whole pack set off at full speed amid the trees, and were lost to sight.

The heat grew more intense than ever, not a breath of wind was stirring, the thunder roared in the distance, gradually the sky, as he could see it through the branches, became of an inky blackness, till a dark pall collected overhead, then the clouds appeared to break up, and whirled round and round each other in a state of dreadful commotion, forked lightening darted from the heavens, and the thunder, in rapid heavy peals, roared and rattled again and again till the very trees of the forest seemed to shake with the concussion. Far away out of the forest arose a black cone-shaped column, which soon joined itself to the mass of clouds overhead, the lightening flashing with greater vividness and rapidity, the thunder becoming more deafening than ever. The sound increased to a dreadful roar, coming nearer and nearer. He had no doubt that it was indeed a whirlwind sweeping through the forest, he could hear the tree tops dashed together, the rending branches, the crashing of falling trees, as the stout branches were twisted round and round, torn up by the roots, or snapped off as if they had been mere saplings. Should the devastating tempest pass across where he stood, he could scarcely hope to avoid being crushed by the falling trees.

He now remembered an open space a short distance off, which, had the ground not been swampy, he would have selected for his camp. He hurried towards it. As he made his way through the forest he could hear behind him those dreadful sounds which betokened the rapid approach of the hurricane. Already the tree tops were waving furiously above his head, as he sprang out into the open space, towards which he was directing his steps. In an instant after the tall trees came crashing down, and almost lifted off his feet, he found himself encircled by masses of leaves and boughs torn off and whirled through the air. On he sped till he gained the centre of the meadow, when, on looking back, a wide opening appeared in the part of the forest through which he had lately passed. An avenue had been formed nearly two hundred yards in width, in which not a tree remained standing, while it seemed to extend far away into the depths of the forest.

As he was anxious to continue his journey, as soon as all was quiet, he set off in the direction taken

by the newly formed avenue. He had to proceed
a considerable distance towards the track which led
to the township, and he kept as near it as the fallen
trees would allow, that he might observe the havoc
which had been produced. He calculated, as he
walked along, that upwards of three miles of forest
had been levelled of the width already mentioned,
and that many thousand trees had, in a few seconds,
been destroyed.

CHAPTER VIII

Donald resuming his journey, hears a cry of distress.—Finds a man under a fallen tree, who, after carrying him some distance, he discovers to be Alec Galbraith.—They camp for the night.

ONALD was about to leave the scene of havoc caused by the whirlwind, when a groan, as if from a person in pain, reached his ears. It was repeated with a faint cry of ' Help! help !' He made his way among the fallen branches in the direction from whence the sound came. At length he saw, beneath a fallen tree, a man of strong frame, so pressed down by a bough that he could not extricate himself.

' Get me out of this, for I can endure the agony no longer,' cried the man.

Donald hastened up to him. ' I'll do my best to release you, my friend ; but let me see how I can best manage it,' he said. At first he thought of chopping away the bough, but then he saw that the man would suffer by the blows. He soon, on examination, determined how alone it could be done. With his axe he cut two pieces of wood, one of which would serve as a crowbar, the other thicker and shorter, to place under the bough after he had raised it. It was a work of time, and his heart was grieved at the pain which the poor man was enduring during the operation.

At length, by great exertion, he raised the bough sufficiently off the crushed limb to enable him to drag out the sufferer.

' Water! water!' were the only words the latter could utter. Donald had a small quantity in a flask, with which he moistened his lips. It somewhat revived the man ; but how, in his crippled state, he could be conveyed to the township, was now the question. The stranger was strongly built and heavy, and Donald felt that, sturdy as he himself was, he could scarcely hope to carry him along the uneven track so great a distance. Still, to leave him in his present exhausted condition was not to be thought of ; the wolves, too, from which he had escaped, might come back before he could possibly return with assistance.

' I must take you on my back, my friend,' he said to the stranger, who appeared to have recovered sufficiently to understand him. ' I see no other way of preserving your life. Trust to me. I can at all events carry you some distance before night-fall, we will then encamp, and continue our journey to-morrow.'

' I am not worth the exertion and trouble it must cause you,' said the man, gloomily. ' The pain overcame me, and I would that the trunk itself

had fallen on me, and put me out of existence altogether.'

'Nay, nay, my friend,' answered Donald. 'You
should rather be thankful to the merciful God who,
though He has allowed you to suffer injury, has preserved your life, that you may yet have an opportunity of devoting it to His service.'

'I do not comprehend your philosophy. I know
that I have been suffering unspeakable agony. I
have nothing to be thankful for on that account,'
answered the man.

'We will not dispute the point now, my friend,'
said Donald. 'But let us make the best of our way
to the township. This stout stick, which I used as
crowbar, will serve to support me as I walk. Now
let me lift you on my shoulders, and we will proceed
on our journey.'

Donald, on this, stooped down, and placed himself so that the stranger could cling to his back, and
with his heavy weight he made his way through the
forest.

He had not gone far, however, before he began
to fear that he should make but slow progress, even
should he not be compelled to abandon his inten-
tions altogether, and to leave the unhappy sufferer
by himself in the forest. He staggered on till he
reached a small stream, where he could obtain water
to quench the sufferer's burning thirst. He examined also the injured limb—the bone did not

appear to be broken, although the flesh was fearfully bruised and discoloured.

The day was already far advanced, and when in a short time he began to feel the strain which had been put on his own muscles, he came to the resolution of encamping where they were, and should no one appear, to continue the journey the next day.

Having first bathed the sufferer's leg in the cold waters of the stream, and bound it up as he best could, he commenced making preparations for encamping, by cutting some spruce fir tops for a bed, collecting stakes and slabs of birch bark to form a hut, and dry branches for a fire. This did not take him long. He hurried through the work, for he wished to shoot some birds or catch some fish for supper. Having lighted a fire, he left his patient, suffering less apparently than before, and went off up the stream hoping to find the necessary provisions.

He was more successful even than he expected, and returned with an ample supply of fish and fowl. Hitherto the stranger had been in too much pain to speak more than a few words. The food greatly revived him ; and as he sat up, leaning against the side of the hut, Donald observed that his eyes were fixed on him with an inquiring look. Donald had spoken several times in broad Scotch.

' It must be so,' exclaimed the stranger at length, ' though I am not surprised, Donald Morrison, that you do not know me.'

Donald gazed eagerly at the stranger's countenance, then leaning forward, grasped his hand.

'Yes, I know you now, Alec Galbraith, my dear friend,' he exclaimed, 'though till this moment I had no suspicion who you were. How thankful I am that I should have been sent to your help.'

Donald then told Alec how anxiously he had been inquiring for him, and how sorry he had been at being unable to discover where he was. 'I don't like to make you talk now, though,' he added. 'You must tell me all about yourself by-and-by.'

'That would not take long, Donald,' answered Alec. 'Though, as the subject is not a pleasant one, I will gladly defer it. Just before I had discovered who you were I had been intending to insist on your leaving me till you could send some one back from the township to bring me in, if any one could be found to perform so thankless an office for a wretched pauper like me. I had been counting on my strong arm and resolution to make my way in the backwoods, as many another determined fellow has done, and now I find myself suddenly brought down, and for what I can tell to the contrary, a helpless cripple for life.'

'You are right in supposing that I would not leave you, my dear Alec,' answered Donald gently. 'Indeed, I would not have done so had you been a stranger. Trust to God's loving mercy for the future. Your leg is not, I hope, materially injured,

and on your recovery you may be able to carry out
the plan you proposed, for I feel sure you will find
employment for your head as well as your arm, and
the two together, in this magnificent country, will
secure you all you can require. But oh, Alec, if
you would but put faith in the love of God and His
protecting care you would no longer be in dread of
the future.'

Alec sat silent for some minutes. 'If God is
such as I was always taught to suppose Him, He can
only visit with His vengeance a being like myself,
who has dared His power, and done numberless
things which He is said to prohibit. No, I feel
that I am a wretched outcast sinner in His sight,
worthy only of punishment. He has for some time
past been pursuing me with His vengeance, and I
see no reason why He should stop till He has
crushed me quite.'

'Of course, my dear Alec, you are perfectly
right in your estimation of yourself, and right, too,
with regard to God, if you judge Him as man
judges. His justice demands your punishment, but
His love and mercy would preserve you if you
would accept the plan He has formed for saving you
and restoring you to that favour which you have
justly lost. He asks you to do what you have just
done, to acknowledge yourself a sinner, and now
do what He demands besides, and throw yourself
unreservedly upon Him.'

'Your system is a beautiful one, Donald, but I confess that I cannot comprehend it,' said Alec, with a groan, produced by the pain he was suffering, then he added, in his old careless and somewhat sarcastic tone, 'Tell me, old fellow, is it thoroughly orthodox.'

'It is according to God's word, and that I dare not dispute,' answered Donald. 'And I will pray that His Holy Spirit will make it as clear to your mind, and bring it home to your soul, as He has to mine. We will not, however, talk further now, as it is important that you should get some sleep. I will watch over you, and keep the fire burning, and I hope that to-morrow we shall be able to resume our journey. Before you sleep, dear friend, we will offer up a prayer for God's direction and assistance.'

'As you think fit,' answered Alec, expressing no satisfaction at the proposal.

Donald knelt and prayed, and then read a portion of God's Word. Alec sat listening, but made no remark, though he pressed his friend's hand when he had finished, and then lying down closed his eyes.

As Donald sat by the side of his friend he observed that though his slumbers were troubled he appeared to sleep soundly. He had resolved to carry him till he could get help, though he felt that the task was almost beyond his strength ; but he did not despair. He prayed for that aid he so much needed, and felt sure that it would be sent in the way God might judge best.

The faithful believer does not expect a miracle to be wrought in his favour, but he knows that the Most High, who allows not a sparrow to fall to the ground without knowing it, so orders and arranges all the movements of His creatures, that He accomplishes, by apparently ordinary means, whatever He desires to bring about. Thus when the believer prays he is sure that his prayer will be answered, though it may not be in the way he, in his finite judgment would desire. Resting securely on God's love and mercy, he is sure that all will be ordered aright.

CHAPTER IX.

When encamped, Donald is visited by an Indian, who assists in carrying Alec to the township.—Influenced by the conduct of the Christian Indians and the exhortations of his friends, Alec is brought to acknowledge the truth.—His brother requires his presence in England, to recover his father's property, and he sets off.

DONALD was still reading from his pocket Bible, but had begun to feel somewhat drowsy, when he was fully aroused by seeing a tall figure moving through the forest towards him. As the stranger approached, the light of the fire exhibited a person of a dark countenance, with black hair, in which were stuck a few tall feathers, while his coat and leggings, ornamented with fringe, were of untanned leather. Donald at once knew him to be one of the natives of the land. The Indian approached fearlessly, and sat down beside him.

'I see your fire from my camp,' he said, in tolerable English. 'I white man's friend. Where you go?'

Donald, who knew that the natives in that district were on friendly terms with the settlers, at once told him who he was, and the difficulty in which he was placed.

'I help you,' said the Indian. 'We not far from river. Canoe take up your friend to township.'

The assistance offered was just what Donald had been praying for.

'God has sent you to my help, my friend,' he said to the Indian, 'and I gratefully accept your offer.'

'You know God and His Son Jesus Christ?' asked the Indian.

'I do, my friend, praise His name that He has made Himself known to me.'

'I know and love Him too,' said the Indian. 'He good Master; I wish all my people knew Him and served Him, then they not drink the fire-water, and vanish out of the land, as they are doing.'

Donald grasped the Indian's hand. 'I do, indeed, wish that not only your people, but mine also, were subjects of the Lord,' he said. 'Let us pray that we may have grace to make His name known among them.'

The white man and the red knelt as brothers, side by side, and together offered up their prayers for the conversion of their countrymen.

'Please read God's Word to me,' said the Indian. 'I love to hear it.'

Donald gladly did as he was requested, his companion occasionally asking him questions. It was nearly midnight before the Indian rose to return to his own camp, promising to come back in the morning with some of his people to convey Alec to the river.

Soon after daybreak, he appeared with a litter, which he had had constructed, and a supply of food, in case, as he said, his white brother might require it. Alec had been for some time awake. He did not appear surprised when the Indians arrived.

'I heard you reading to the stranger,' he said, 'but I was too weary to speak.'

As soon as breakfast was over, Alec was placed on the litter, and the Indians bore him along lightly and easily through the forest. It was past noon before the bank of the stream was reached. Here they launched two of their canoes, which together were sufficient to convey the whole party. Alec was placed in one, under charge of the chief, and Donald took his seat in the other. At night they camped on shore, when Donald read the Bible to his redskin friends, Alec being apparently an attentive listener.

'It is strange,' he afterwards remarked to Alec, 'that that book should have such a power over the men of the wilderness as apparently to change their savage natures.'

'God's Holy Spirit is the power applied to those who accept His offer made to them by means of the book,' continued Donald. 'You, my dear Alec, will experience the same change if you will but take God at His word and trust Him, although you, from having had these offers often made and rejected, may have to pass through many troubled waters, such as these children of the desert have not experienced. But remember His words, " Seek and ye shall find, knock and it shall be opened unto you." What encouragement does that promise afford sinners, conscious that they are such, and tossed about with doubts and fears.'

Alec made no reply. Donald, however, felt sure that the conduct and conversation of his Indian friends had had a great effect on his mind.

On the evening of the second day, the party reached the township, when the Indians conveyed Alec to Donald's house. The sincerity of the chief was proved, when he refused to receive any reward for the service he had rendered.

' No, no, my friend,' he answered. ' I rejoice to help brother Christians, for I remember the Lord's words, " I was hungred, and ye gave me meat : I was thirsty, and ye gave me drink : I was a stranger, and ye took me in : naked, and ye clothed me : I was sick, and ye visited me : I was in prison, and ye came unto me." '

Alec, who had been laid on Donald's bed, desired to bid farewell to the Indians before they took their departure, and to thank them for the service they had rendered him.

'Do not speak of it, friend,' answered the Indian. 'Jesus, our Master, went about doing good. I only try to be like Him, and I very, very far away from that.'

'It is wonderful, very wonderful,' murmured Alec, after the Indians had left him. 'I do not think my philosophy could have changed them as their faith in the Bible appears to have done.'

Notwithstanding this, it was long before Donald perceived the desired change in his friend's heart.

The surprise of David may be supposed, when, on his arrival from the office, he found a stranger in the house, and discovered who he was, and though he grieved to see him in so sad a condition, yet he was thankful that he had thus been placed under his and his brother's care. Like brothers, indeed, they watched over him, assisted by Mr Skinner, who, as they had to be constantly absent, proposed taking up his abode with them till Alec's recovery.

'I shall make a capital nurse,' he said, 'and may be able to minister to a mind diseased.'

Donald had also obtained the assistance of a surgeon, who at first seemed very doubtful whether Alec would ever recover the use of his limb, and expressed himself somewhat carelessly to that effect in the hearing of his patient. Alec groaned.

'To be a miserable cripple and a friendless beggar for the rest of my life,' he muttered.

'No, no, dear Alec, you will not be either friend-

less or a beggar,' said David, who sat by his side.
' While Donald and I live you will find means of
employment, even if you lose the use of your leg ;
and I am sure you know enough of us to feel that
we can only rejoice to have you beneath our roof.'

For many days Alec continued ill and feverish,
and seemed to pay but little attention to what Mr
Skinner from time to time said to him, although his
kind friend spoke most judiciously, and always
sought the right season for speaking. He did not
always, indeed, address him directly.

' It seems surprising to me,' he observed, one
day, ' that anyone should fail to acknowledge that
man is composed of two parts, the physical and
spiritual, and that God, his maker, who has so amply
provided for his physical wants, and formed this
world so beautifully and so perfect, should have neglected supplying the wants of his spiritual part—
by far the most important—with what it so greatly
requires, guidance and direction ; and above all
things, what it so yearns after, a knowledge of Him
who formed it. Now those who really study the
book (which professes to be given by God) according to the way He in it points out,—namely, in a
humble spirit,—with prayer for enlightenment—in
variably find that want fully supplied ; and making
due allowance for the various constitutions of the
human mind, they are entirely agreed on all cardinal
points regarding the Bible, while its opponents, who

profess to be guided by the light of reason alone, differ in every possible way, their theories being almost countless; while they agree only in denying the authority of a book, of the Divine nature of which they have no experimental knowledge, declining, in their pride, to follow the directions it gives them for obtaining that knowledge. Then, when we take a glance round the heathen world, past and present, we find men following courses, with habits and customs destructive to human happiness, and abhorrent to the conscience which God has given man when uncontaminated by them. Contrast the result which the theories of philosophers and the heathen systems produced, with that which the mild loving faith Christ taught, if universally adopted, would bring about in the world, and who would hesitate between the two? And then when, in addition, we remember that Christ ensures to His followers eternal happiness, greater even than the mind of man can comprehend, what madness is it in those who hesitate to accept His offers! True, there are mysteries which even the Bible does not explain, such as the existence of Satan; but it does explain why Satan has power over man, and why sin and misery and death came into the world. This was the reason that man was disobedient, that man refused to trust to his Maker and listened to Satan. Man, in the pride of youth, health, and strength, and mental powers, may look

with contempt on the Gospel, but God, in His loving
mercy brings down those He loves, by poverty, suffering, and loss of friends, and then they feel their
weakness and the vanity of all human systems, and
are led to turn to Him who alone can lift them up
and give them comfort, and a promise of a better
life. How plain and easy are the demands He
makes ; how full of mercy ; how simple is the plan
He has arranged.'

Alec, as usual, had had been listening attentively
to all Mr Skinner had said. He never attempted
to argue with him. He had long lost all confidence
in the correctness of the notions he had held. Tears
filled his eyes. 'I believe, help Thou my unbelief,'
he ejaculated, in a broken voice.

His health and strength had been rapidly im-
proving. Through the assistance of his friends,
when perfectly recovered, he obtained employment,
and was soon able to lay by money, and to feel himself independent. Notwithstanding this, by his life
and conversation, he showed that the good seed had
taken root ; the only companionship he sought was
that of Donald and David, and Mr Skinner, and
other true Christians whom he could meet with in the
neighbourhood. He had followed his friends' example, and purchased a piece of land, which he had
commenced cultivating, and on which he told them
he hoped soon to put up a substantial log-house.

'You will not like to live a solitary life,' said

Donald. ' You will want a companion. I did not get on half as well as I do now before David came out.'

' Perhaps I may some day find one,' answered Alec, smiling. ' I shall live on in hopes that one of congenial tastes to my own may be sent me.'

' Till you find him you must promise to remain on with us,' said Donald. We cannot part with you, and I suspect that we should be jealous of any one whom you might select.'

A short time after this Alec received a letter from one of his long absent brothers, who had returned to England. He wrote saying that he had looked into their father's affairs, and found that there was yet some property which might be recovered, but that it would require his presence and that of the rest of the family, to settle the matter. A remittance, to enable him, without inconvenience, to pay his passage home, was enclosed in the letter. Donald and David were truly glad to hear of this.

' You must not be persuaded, Alec, however, to stay away,' they exclaimed. ' You must promise to come back as soon as your affairs are arranged. You are wanted in this country.'

Mr Skinner, while he congratulated his young friend on the brightening of his worldly prospects, cautioned him affectionately against the temptations to which he might be exposed.

'I know that I am very weak,' answered Alec, humbly.   But I go forth, not in my own strength but seeking the aid and direction of God's Holy Spirit.'

'While that is sought, and it will never be de-denied, you will be strong, and I have no fear of the result,' was the answer.

The Morrisons and Mr Skinner undertook to look after Alec's property during his absence, and he set off on his journey to England.

CHAPTER X.

A letter from Margaret.—Janet's illness.—Anxiety about Alec's
return.—A delightful surprise.—Arrival of Alec and Margaret with Janet.—Margaret has become Alec's wife.—Conducted by the brothers to their new house.—Arrival of Mr
Skinner's sister, Mrs Ramsden and her daughters, who, as
might possibly be expected, become the wives of Donald
and David.—Janet continuing to live with Margaret, pays
frequent visits to her other bairns, and is ever welcomed
by them, and the numerous wee bairns who spring up in
their midst.—Conclusion.

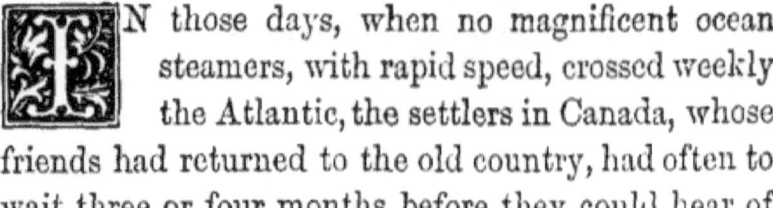I N those days, when no magnificent ocean
steamers, with rapid speed, crossed weekly
the Atlantic, the settlers in Canada, whose
friends had returned to the old country, had often to
wait three or four months before they could hear of
their safe arrival.

Some time after Alec had gone a letter was received from Margaret, written in a less happy strain
than was usual to her. Janet had been suffering
from rheumatism, and found it impossible to spin
as much as she had been accustomed to do. The
state of her health made her feel an unwonted
anxiety about the future prospects of her beloved
charge. 'I know, however, that all will be well.'

116

wrote Margaret, ' so I do my best to keep up her
spirits, by reminding her of God's loving kindness,
in which she has hitherto so firmly confided.   Were
it not, however, for the assistance you have given
us, my dear brothers, I confess that we should have
a great difficulty in supporting ourselves.   I do all
I can to repay our kind and loving friend for the
years of tender care she has bestowed on us.
What would have become of us all had it not been
for her ?'

Donald and David had a short time before this
sent home a larger sum than usual, which they
hoped would have been received soon after the
letter was written, and they trusted that it would
assist to restore Janet's spirits, and convince her
that as long as they lived Margaret would not be
left destitute.

Weeks and weeks passed by, and no acknowledgment of the sum was received, and no other
letter came to hand.

As they hoped that Alec Galbraith would not
be long absent, wishing to give him a pleasant surprise, they had gone on with the erection of his
house, and completed it, declaring that as their reward they would sell their property, for which they
had had several advantageous offers, and go and live
with him till they should fix on another location
further off in the wilderness, to bring under cultiva-
tion.

'He must have been at home several weeks, and had plenty of time to arrange his affairs with his brothers,' observed David.

'I wonder he has not written to us. Perhaps the letter, or the vessel herself bringing it, may have been lost,' observed Donald. 'That has been the fate of several of Margaret's letters. Depend upon it we shall hear from him or our sister before long, and he is sure to pay her a visit before he comes back, that he may bring us news of her and Janet.'

They were seated together one evening in their log house, their meal just placed on the table. 'I fancy I heard footsteps,' said David. 'Yes, some one hails.'

It was Alec Galbraith's voice. Donald and David rushed out. There stood Margaret and Alec Galbraith, while dear old Janet followed with eager looks close behind them. Donald, seizing his sister's hands, drew her to him, while David grasped those of Alec, till his brother could relinquish Margaret to him, and then kind Janet, rushing forward, threw her arms around both the brother's necks, and sobbed out, 'My bairns, my bairns, though I feared the salt sea I would have gone over more than twice the distance to hold ye thus agen!'

The new arrivals were soon seated at the already spread board. As Margaret happened to place her hand on the table Donald observed a plain gold ring on her finger.

'What!' he exclaimed, turning quickly to Alec. 'Is it really so?'

'I thought we should surprise you,' he answered, laughing. 'But I would not come away without her, and as she knew that you would mourn my absence, she at last consented to return with me as my wife, provided Janet would come also. It was a hard matter, however, I can assure you, to persuade her to venture across the ocean.'

'Indeed, my dear Donald,' said Margaret, when she and her brother were shortly afterwards together, and her husband was absent, 'much as I found I loved him, and had loved him since I was a girl, I would not have consented to be his wife had I not been convinced that he had abandoned those infidel principles which had caused his poor mother so much grief, and had also become a faithful follower of the Lord. I was at first delighted to see him, and then my heart sank within me for fear that he was unchanged. He did not leave me long in doubt on the subject. I knew by his gentle and subdued manners, by the unmistakable expressions he used, and then by the deep sorrow that he expressed, that the opinions he once held had grieved his poor mother, that he no longer adhered to the vain philosophy in which he had formerly gloried. I soon discovered that he loved me, and then I had no hesitation in giving him my heart in return.'

'You acted wisely and rightly, dear Margaret and David and I are truly glad to welcome him as a brother, whom we have long looked upon as the most intimate of our friends.'

The next day, Alec and Margaret, accompanied by Janet, were conducted in due form by Donald and David to the house which they had but lately finished on Alec's property. The surprise was indeed a great and delightful one. As it did not take long to get in as much furniture as was required at that season of the year, Margaret and her husband, with her faithful nurse, in a few days took up their abode there.

Alec's worldly circumstances had greatly improved, for much more of his father's property had been recovered than he expected, so that his share was considerable, and with the experience he had gained, he was able to employ his capital in farming, with great advantage.

'What will you two poor bachelors do by yourselves,' said Margaret. 'Could you not manage to come and live with us in this house as you purposed doing had Alec returned alone?'

'We have work enough in drawing our plans, and other business of our office to employ nearly every hour of the day,' answered Donald. 'And besides, we are anxious to assist Mr Skinner, who wishes to enlarge his house as soon as possible, as he expects a widowed sister and her family to join him shortly, and he does not consider the accommodation he can now offer them, sufficient.'

'Oh, I suppose he wishes to have a nursery built where the children may be out of hearing,' said Margaret, laughing.

'He has not mentioned the ages of his nieces, or how many there are of them,' said David, 'but I should think, from a remark he made, that they cannot be little children.'

The young men made no inquiry of their friend about the more juvenile portion of the family of his expected relatives. As he had himself now been some time absent from England, he might have been able to give them very little information. David, however, confessed to Margaret that he felt somewhat curious on the subject. This was increased when the new part of the house having been finished, Mr Skinner fitted up one chamber which he said was for his sister, and two other pretty little rooms for his elder nieces, and certainly the furniture, which he put in to them, was scarcely such as he would have chosen for young children.'

Just at the time Mr Skinner was expecting the arrival of his sister, Mrs Ramsden and her family, Donald and David had to leave home to visit some distant township on business. Mr Skinner had, before this asked the assistance of Margaret and Janet in fitting up his house. Janet, with her

usual kindness of heart, offered to remain for a day
or two to receive the new comers, whom she under-
stood had no servant with them.

'The poor lady may be tired, and the bairns
will ha' na one to gie them their supper, and put
them to bed, and it will be just like old times
coming back, and be a muckle pleasure to me,' she
observed, to Margaret. Mr Skinner was very glad
to accept her services, feeling sure that she would
be of much assistance, although he might not have
supposed that his nieces would require the attend-
ance of a nurse.

Janet was to bring word to Margaret when
Mrs Ramsden would be able to see her, and she
proposed then walking over with Alec to visit
her.

She had numberless occupations which kept her
and Janet fully employed; for though her husband
had engaged a sturdy Scotch girl to milk the cows,
and perform some of the rougher work of the farm,
the damsel herself required her constant superin-
tendence. There were poultry of several varieties,
as well as pigs, to be fed; the flower and kitchen
garden to be cultivated, and numerous household
duties to be attended to, Alec himself being constantly engaged in clearing fresh ground, and in the
more laborious work about the farm.

Margaret had greatly missed Janet the days she
had been absent, and with much satisfaction, there-

fore, she saw her with her knitting in hand—without which, even in Canada, she never moved abroad —approaching the house.

Oh yes, they are come, my bairn,' she said, to Margaret's inquiry. ' Mistress Ramsden herself is a brave lady, and seldom have my eyes rested on twa mair bonny lassies than her daughters, na pride, na nonsense about the young leddies, Mistress Mary and Emily Ramsden, and just as gentle, and loving, and kind as lambs to the younger children. They thanked me for my help ; but they put their hands to everything themselves, and would nae let me do half as much as I wished. I'll tell you what, Margaret, I have set my heart on having them for my twa bairns. They would make them bonny wives, indeed, but don't ye gang and tell your brothers, for there is that obstinacy in human nature that they might back, and kick, and run off into the woods rather than do what, if left alone, they would be eager after.'

Margaret promised to be discreet, and allow her brothers to judge for themselves, without praising the Misses Ramsden, should her opinion of them, as she had little doubt it would agree with that formed by Janet. Next morning she and Alec paid their promised visit, and she was fully as much disposed as Janet to admire the Misses Ramsden and their mother. The more she saw of them the more pleased she was, not only with their appearance, but with their earnest piety, their simple unassuming manners, and their apparent energy and determination, and their evident readiness to submit to all the inconveniences to which settlers in a new country must, of necessity, be subjected.

A few days after this Donald and David returned, and called on Margaret on their way home. They naturally inquired whether Mrs Ramsden and her family had arrived. She wisely said but little about the young ladies, and Janet was equally discreet. They, however, managed to find their way that evening to Mr Skinner's.

They were always glad to pay their kind friend a visit; but from their sister's and Janet's discreet silence, they suspected that the change in the character of his establishment would be a drawback to the pleasure of their previous intercourse. Not, however, till a much later hour than usual on the evening in question did they discover that it was high time to take up their hats and wish Mr Skinner and his sister and her daughters good-bye.

As they walked homewards, Donald, after a long silence, burst out laughing, exclaiming, 'Weel, I expected to see a number of bairns in pinafores, but eh ! she's a braw lassie.'

'She is the sweetest young creature I have ever had the happiness of meeting,' said David.

'But I am talking of the elder sister,' exclaimed Donald.

'And I speak of the younger,' observed David. 'But they are both very nice girls—there is no doubt as to that—no nonsense about them—so full of spirits and fun, and yet so lady-like and quite, and I heard Emily's voice, when joining in the prayer, it was so true and earnest.'

'I was nearest Mary, and was struck by the genuine tone of her's,' observed Donald.

'Do you know, David, that I had made up my mind to follow the example of Mr Skinner, and to live a bachelor for ten years to come at least, and then, perhaps, to go back to the old country to look out for a wife. But eh! that looking out for a wife must be unsatisfactory work at best. How can a man possibly discover the real character and dis- position of a lady when the object he has in view is suspected, if not well known.'

'We may be sure we shall be guided aright if we seek guidance in that as in all other matters,' answered David. 'But I cannot help hoping that neither you nor I need be compelled to make the expedition you suggest. I have sought guidance, and I am sure that in God's good time we shall be directed aright.'

Day after day, when their work was over, they had some cogent reason for calling at their friend's house ; and when Margaret next met them, Donald confessed that if he ever could venture to marry he should be thankful to make Mary Ramsden his wife, while David made the same acknowledgment with regard to her younger sister.

Happily, in a prosperous country like Canada, to steady and industrious men like the young Morrisons, the impediments were not insuperable, nor, indeed, did they take long to overcome.

Faithful Janet was overjoyed when she heard that the lassies she so much admired had promised to become the wives of her twa bairns, with a full approval of their mother and uncle. As they agreed that their old house might not always be sufficiently large to hold them both, they moved further off to the west, where they were enabled to purchase, by the sale of their already well cultivated farm, two good sized allotments of land, on each of which they reared a comfortable log house, where, shortly afterwards, they and their brides took up their abode.

'My work is among my fellow-creatures,' observed Mr Skinner, 'or I should be much inclined, my dear nephews, to follow your example, and move nearer you.

He therefore remained at the now well advanced township, though before long, to their great satisfaction, the Galbraiths became their near neighbours, Alec having purchased a property a little beyond theirs.

The Morrisons gratefully remembered the kindness they had received from Mr M'Tavish and other friends in the old country. To many young men who came out with introductions from them they gave a hearty welcome, extending a helping hand to those who required assistance, while they rendered a still greater service to not a few whom they saw falling into evil ways, by perseveringly, though gently and lovingly, warning and exhorting them—not leaving them in spite of ingratitude and opposition, till they had been the means of bringing them back into the right path.

In the latter respect especially, Alec followed their example. He remembered into what a depth of sin he had sunk, and that it was through the love of Jesus, and by no merit of his own, he was drawn out of it. His sin he knew was washed away. Gratitude to that loving Saviour urged him to try and call those sheep who were wandering away along the thorny paths he had followed into the true fold, where they might rest secure under charge of the faithful Shepherd who never forsakes those who seek Him.

Janet, though continuing to live with Margaret, paid frequent visits to the other houses of the family, at which her coming was always hailed with delight by the numerous wee bairns, who, in the course of time, made their appearance among them, as she was also warmly welcomed by Donald and David, who, though they felt that to Mr Skinner they were, humanly speaking, indebted for the spiritual life they enjoyed, could never forget how devotedly she had watched over their infancy and youth, and that it was mainly to her training and instruction their present prosperity was owing.